American Music: Born in the USA

A History of American Music

Kathleen Walls

First edition, 2024 © Kathleen Walls
All rights reserved.
No part of this book may be produced in any form, by photocopying or by any electronic or mechanical means, including information storage or retrieval systems, without permission in writing from both the copyright owner and the publisher of this book, except for the minimum words needed for review.
Disclaimer Notice:
Please note the information contained within this book is for educational and entertainment purposes only. All effort has been made to verify the accuracy of the information. No warranties of any kind are declared or implied.

ISBN: 978-0-9861109-7-9
Library of Congress Control Number: 2023951801

Published by Global Authors Publications
Filling the GAP in publishing

Edited by Renee S. Gordon and P. W. Aide
Interior Design by Kathleen Walls
Cover Design by Kathleen Walls
Front Cover Art by Kathleen Walls

Published in Sedelia, MO and Middleburg, FL, USA for Global Authors Publications

Other Books by Kathleen Walls
Nonfiction
Wild About Florida: South Florida

Wild About Florida: North Florida

Wild About Florida: Central Florida

Finding Florida's Phantoms

Hosts With Ghosts

Georgia's Ghostly Getaways

Manhunt: The Eric Rudolph Story

Fiction
Last Step

Kudzu

Missing-- Gone but not Forgotten

The Tenant from Hell

Double Duplicity

The Ranch House Heist

Dedication

This book is dedicated to the memory of my grandmother, Mamie "Nannie" Mullen Shereck, my mother, Mary Rita Shereck Reugger, and my father, Robert Joseph "Pop" Reugger. They were the ones who first introduced me to music and began my lifelong love of it.

Acknowledgement

I need to thank all the convention and visitors bureau and public relations people who helped me visit the many shrines to American music. Without them, I could never have written this book.

I also want to thank my friends Renee Gordon, Kathy Barnett, and the many museum curators, CVB, and PR people for their helpful advice in checking the accuracy of my information. Special thanks to Emily Epley, Travel and Tourism Director of Cleveland County, NC and Kim Smith, Marketing Director for Heart of Appalachia in Virginia, who went way beyond basics with their help.

Table of Contents

Introduction: They Brought the Seeds 1

Chapter 1 Personal Music Roots   3
Chapter 2 Roots Run Deep   5
Chapter 3 Music in the Fields   11
Chapter 4 Cajun and Zydeco 14
Chapter 5 Blues 21
Chapter 6 Ragtime   39
Chapter 7 Jazz   44
Chapter 8 Bebop 51
Chapter 9 Women in Jazz   59
Chapter 10 Country   68
Chapter 11 Western Music   98
Chapter 12 Women in Country Music   104
Chapter 13 Bluegrass 118
Chapter 14 The Outlaw movement   122
Chapter 15 Gospel   135
Chapter 16 R&B and Soul   141
Chapter 17 Motown   157
Chapter 18 Rock and Roll   164
Chapter 19 Folk Music and Protest Era 190
Chapter 20 Muscle Shoals Sound   204
Chapter 21 Southern Rock   207
Chapter 22 Pop   213

Introduction: They Brought the Seeds

When early settlers came to America they often brought few material items, but they brought many customs, traditions, and music of their homeland here. These things, mainly the music took root in America's soil and grew.

These emigrants came for many different reasons. Some came to escape poverty and find a better life. Many were forced out of their homeland by war. There were many who had no choice but were torn from their families and homes and brought here.

Unlike some versions of history state, this was not a land someone had "discovered." There were indigenous groups with established cultures who had lived here for thousands of years. In spite of the misconception that all Indians wore feathers, lived in teepees, and had the same culture, Native American music and culture differed regionally and from tribe to tribe. They each had their own music as well.

America really was a melting pot then. The music of Native Americans, white settlers, and the Black enslaved people mingled to create new forms and songs from Delta blues and "hillbilly" music, to rock. My biggest question is does the music reflect the culture, or does the culture reflect the music?

This is the history of American music. It's the music of the people. There are many others who helped shape American music, but I know I can't get every musician and event that I would like to or this book would go on forever, but I tried to get the ones I feel made the biggest impact. Forgive me if I missed one of your favorites.

From its birth in the 1700s through the 1970s. As you look at the history of music, you look at American history. It's not always a pretty story. Sometimes labor pains are hard, but in the end, it shouts loud and clear, "I was Born in the USA!"

Chapter 1 Personal Music Roots

Music was part of my life from my earliest memories. My mom and my grandmother, Nannie to me, played piano and sang some of the old, mostly Irish ballads. One favorite was "When Irish Eyes are Smiling." It dates back to 1912, but the version sung by Irish tenor John McCormack during the First World War was popular. The song says:

>When Irish eyes are smiling,
>Sure it's like a morn in Spring,
>In the lilt of Irish laughter
>You can hear the angels sing.
>When Irish hearts are happy,
>All the world seems bright and gay,
>And when Irish eyes are smiling,
>Sure, they steal your heart away.

Another popular song they often played and sang was "I'll Take You Home Again, Kathleen," a song with German-American origins, but often mistaken for an Irish ballad.

>Oh! I will take you back, Kathleen
>To where your heart will feel no pain
>And when the fields are fresh and green
>I'll take you to your home again!

My parents named me for one of those old songs. "Kathleen Mavourneen" written in 1837, with lyrics by a Mrs. Crawford. "Mavourneen" in the Irish language, Gaelic, means "my beloved,"

>Oh have you forgotten how soon we must sever?
>Oh have you forgotten this day we must part?
>It may be for years and it may be forever
>Oh why art thou silent thou voice of my heart?
>It may be for years and it may be forever;
>Then art thou silent Kathleen Mavourneen?

My dad had his favorites, too. Since he was a big baseball fan and played shortstop for a minor league New Orleans team for a while, it's not surprising he loved "Take Me out to the Ball Game."

Another song he would do a routine with was "I Found a Million Dollar Baby in a Five and Ten Cent Store." I'm not sure which version he was mimicking as it was recorded by Bing Crosby and by Victor Young's orchestra with vocal by The Boswell Sisters in 1931. Benny Goodman recorded it in 1941, and Dizzy Gillespie in 1950. I was born in 1942 when jazz and big band music was at its height in New Orleans and I remember Pop doing his routine when I was pretty young, so probably he was copying one of the earlier versions. The way it went was he would sing the first line about finding a million dollar baby in a five and ten cent store. Then he would stop and shake his head and tell my brother and I, "They don't have those any more."

We would always ask, "What don't they have, million dollar babies?"

He would reply, "No. Five and ten cents stores."

In my later years as a travel writer, music took on a more personal touch. Touching the well where Loretta Lynn drew water and meeting Naomi Judd's mother gave me an insight into the lives of these women. I interviewed Lum York about his years as one of Hank Williams' Drifting Cowboys. Holding the Sun Studio mike Elvis, Johnny Cash, and Jerry Lee Lewis recorded with was a thrill. I visited many of the places that are part of American music history. These close encounters with music led me to write this book to help preserve one of America's greatest heritages, its history of music.

Chapter 2 Roots Run Deep

The seeds of American music sprouted from old home stock. Even before the American Revolution, settlers were beginning to filter into the mountains of Appalachia. The children of those settlers, heard their parents singing songs from their homeland. These songs remained in their hearts and morphed into slightly different music as they reached adulthood. Unlike me, some of those children had musical talent and created new songs that better fit their new land.

England was the most powerful country on earth then. King James displaced Catholic Irish and took their land in the name of the crown. He sent Scotsmen to farm his new plantations in Ireland. Some of the expelled Irish settled in American, and drifted into the least populated areas, the mountains of Appalachia.

The Scots sent to Ireland by the king could never own the land in Ireland. Eventually, many of them who had adsorbed many Irish customs and became know as Scots-Irish, drifted to America. After the Revolution, Washington and the new government wanted to repay the men who fought so hard to create this new country. There was no money in the treasury, so Congress authorized bounty-land warrants for military service in the Revolutionary War under acts of 1788, 1803, and 1806. Enlisted men got 100 acres. Of course, the least desirable farm land was the mountains of Appalachia. These settlers brought with them the music of Ireland and Scotland.

When I lived in Blairsville, Georgia, I attended the Friday night music at the Old Courthouse. Local and visiting musicians played and sang many old Appalachian ballads. One night I was amazed to hear a song my Irish grandmother, Mamie Mullen Shereck, used to play on her piano and sing when I was little. She told me she learned it from her grandmother. My grandmother was born in 1871. Her mother, Mary Devlin Mullen, was born in County Galway, Ireland in 1852 and her mother, Ellen Hagens Devlin, was born in

1820 and migrated to America in the 1860s. No telling how old the song was when she learned it. According to Wiltshire and Swindon History Center, the song was popular throughout the Thames Valley. There is also a Scotch version dated 1769, and there's a copy in *Bell's Songs of the English Peasantry*.

The verse I most remembered was:
> I came in the other night drunk as I could be.
> Saw somebody's shoes under the bed where my shoes ought to be.
> I says to her, 'wife dear wife,
> Whose shoes are under the bed where my shoes ought to be?'
> 'You drunk fool, you blind fool, you surely cannot see.
> It's nothing but a chamber pot my granny gave to me.'
> 'I've traveled this wide world many times, and I'll travel it many more.
> But I've never seen a chamber pot with shoelaces in before.'

There seems to be dozens of variations on this same theme. It's these variations that created American music from the songs of the old country. A song still sung today all across the country that originally came from Scotland is *Auld Lang Syne*. The words were first put in writing by the Scottish poet, Robert Burns, in 1788. Burns admitted it was an old folk song and claimed he, "took it down from an old man." We are all familiar with the first verse and chorus. And have no problem realizing *auld* is the Scottish version of "old." Likewise, *Lang Syne* means "long time." A cup of kindness in Scotland would have meant a cup of tea.

> Should auld acquaintance be forgot,
> And never brought to mind?
> Should auld acquaintance be forgot,
> And auld lang syne
>
> **Chorus**
> For auld lang syne, my dear,
> For auld lang syne.
> We'll take a cup o' kindness yet,
> For auld lang syne.

Another song a group sang one Friday night at the Blairsville Courthouse concert was called *Bonny Barbara Allen*. They did the old traditional version that was once sung in England, Ireland, and Scotland first.

O hooly, hooly rofe flie up,
To the place where he was lying',
And when fhe drew the curtain by,
Young man, I think you're dying.
O its I'm Tick, and very very fick,
And 'tis a' for Barbara Allan.
O the better for me ye's never be,
Tho' your heart's blood were a fpilling.
O dinna ye mind, young man, laid lie,
When ye was in the tavern a drinking,
That ye made the healths gae round and round,
And flighted Barbara Allan. :
He turn'd his face unto the wall,
And death was with him dealing.,
Adieu, adieu, my dear friends all,
And be kind to Barbara Allan.
And -flowly, flowly raife (he up,
And flowly, flowly left him;
And iighing, aid, he cou'd not May,
Since death of life had reft him.
She had not gane a mile but twa,
When lie beard the "dead-bell ringing?
And ev'ry jow that the dead-bell gied,
It cry'd, Woe to Barbara Allan,
O mother, mother, make my bed,
O make It faft and narrow,
Since my love died for me to-day,
I'll die for him to-morrow.

This version is difficult and almost requires a translation. "F" and "t" were where we would use "s" as in "fhe,""tick" and "flighted," rather than "she," "sick," and "sighted." The earliest print version was a 1690 broadside published in London as "Barbara Allen's cruelty."

The newer version they sang was done in modern English and easily understood. It's been recorded in modern times by widely different musicians. Dolly Parton and the Irish group, Altan, who put in some of the original Gallic version, recorded it in 1994. There were versions by Bob Dylan, Joan Baez, Emmy Lou Harris, and dozens of other singers. A perfect example of American music created from adapting older songs brought here by immigrants.

Settlers in the Appalachians lived in log cabins built with their own hands. Most of their possessions were crafted by hand. Woman gathered together and made quilts from scraps of discarded clothing. They used ashes and fat from the hogs to make soap. Wax from beehives made candles to light the cabins. Clothing was made from old feed sacks. Blacksmiths made sturdy iron tools and kitchen utensils.

The few items these people bought were basic necessities. Pianos were far too large and expensive to bring to their new homes. The violin was smaller, and many brought one with them to this county. Both the Irish and the Scottish people share a rich history of fiddle music. As they played it in the evenings sitting on the porch, the music was different. It became known as a fiddle and was used to accompany the adapted folk songs of the mountains. The songs were modified and became a different version than the original. They were Americanized.

One place to get a taste of life in those days is at Mountain Life Museum in Blairsville. It's just a block off the Square and housed in the Grapelle Butt Mock House. The house, built around 1906, contains many objects belong to the Butt family. The home offers a glimpse of how a middle-class family lived in Blairsville in the early 20th century. Outside you see an earlier time with the relocated 1861 Payne Cabin, and a barn, corn-crib and smithy; practically an entire early settlers' village is built around the cabin. The county hosts a Mountain Heritage Festival there Labor Day weekend showcasing the old time music and arts and crafts of the mountain people.

Trees were plentiful and around the early 1800s, someone devised a new instrument, the dulcimer. They were small enough to lay in the lap or on a table and play. The dulcimers had three or four strings. They often made frets from scraps of wire they used on the farm.

By the mid-1800s, another instrument became synonymous with Appalachian music, the banjo. The banjo didn't come from Europe. It originated in West Africa and was brought to this country by enslaved people. This new instrument helped create the Americanized music both here in the mountains and on the Southern plantations.

"Aunt" Samantha Bumgarner and **Eva Davis** made a recording using the five-string banjo in 1924 leading the way into country music. Those early recordings were "Shout Lou," "Fly Around My Pretty Lil' Miss," and "Cindy in the Meadow."

If you want to get an authentic feel for the old music of Appalachia, there are a few places it still lives. Blairsville, Georgia's Old Courthouse has concerts on Friday night May through October. There is also a museum in the courthouse recounting the old history.

Vogel State Park has Music in the Park every Saturday in the summer.

Dahlonega's Bear on the Square Mountain Festival held in April has a lot of the old music being played.

The Blue Ridge Institute & Museum in Ferrum, Virginia holds an annual Crooked Road Dulcimer Festival in August.

Floyd's General Store in Floyd, Virginia is another place to experience authentic Appalachian music. It is home to a group of musicians and dancers who are carrying on the tradition of their families.

Sam Ensley and Cain't Hardly Playboys at Blairsville Courthouse

*(Top) Musicians and Clog Dancer at Bear on the Square, Dahlonega
(Bottom) Display of old mountain music instruments at Dr. Ralph Stanley Museum in Clintwood, VA*

Chapter 3 Music in the Fields

Some of the people who shaped American music didn't come willingly. In August 1619, they brought 20 to 30 enslaved Africans into Hampton, Virginia aboard the English privateer ship *White Lion*. A few days later, a second ship, *Treasurer*, arrived with more enslaved Africans. They were taken from the Spanish slave ship *San Juan Bautista* by the English privateers and are the first recorded Africans to arrive in England's American colonies.

They were not the first Africans in what is now the United States. In 1565, Pedro Menéndez de Avilés established St. Augustine, he brought both free and enslaved Africans here.

Most enslaved Africans in what is now United States came from West Central Africa. They brought their culture with them, including instruments common in their country, the banjo and drums. They also brought the culture of music to tell every day stories. In Africa, they celebrated life events in song.

American Banjo Museum in Oklahoma City tells the banjo story from its African roots to the Jazz Age and is home of the American Banjo Museum Hall of Fame. On the Southern plantation, the banjo remained rooted in African traditions. White owners saw the drum as dangerous and banned it. The enslaved Africans maintained their drum tradition by generating percussion using other devices or their own bodies.

One exception was in New Orleans. The French, which then owned Louisiana, established *Code Noir* in 1724. The Code Noir stated that slaves were to be instructed in the Catholic faith, given food and clothing allowances, allowed to rest on Sundays, and had the right to petition a public prosecutor if they were mistreated. There, enslaved people were allowed to gather in Congo Square on Sundays in their little bit of free time. It was a place where they could meet, sing, and dance to their traditional drums. The Bamboula, a drum made from giant bamboo and covered with a goat skin, is played by beating with fingers and heel of the hand. It was played in Congo Square more than 300 years ago. They still play similar rhythms today in the second-line parades. Congo Square has a bronze sculpture of enslaved people playing drums and dancing.

Another style adopted from African native songs is call and response. The leader, usually someone with a powerful voice and rhythm, would sing the first line. The other slaves would respond and sing the chorus. After the chorus, the leader would sing another solo line and then the group would follow with a chorus. As the enslaved Africans were forced to adopt Christianity, these songs morphed into spirituals with the "preacher" singing the lead.

Frederick Douglas and Harriet Tubman both said that many of the spirituals supposedly sung as religious songs had social meanings hidden from white masters who just heard what they thought were traditional religious songs. For example:

Oh, Mary, don't you weep, don't you mourn
Didn't Pharaoh's army get drowned?
Oh, Mary, don't you weep
Well, Satan got mad and he knows I'm glad
Missed that soul that he thought he had
Now, didn't Pharaoh's army get drowned?

White owners heard a song about Moses and the Israelites' escape from Egypt. Africans knew "Pharaoh" and "Satan" meant "master" and "that soul" referred to one of their people who escaped. Likewise, the song "Wade in the Water," a song whites just took to tell about Israelites crossing the Jordan, reminded those seeking freedom to walk in the rivers along their journey, so that tracking dogs and slave-hunters could not follow their footprints or scent.

Wade in the water, children
Wade in the water
God's gonna trouble the water
God's gonna trouble the water

One song reputed to be used by Underground Railroad workers is "Follow the Drinkin' Gourd." The song supposedly refers to the star formation, the Big Dipper. The Big Dipper aligns with the North Star, instructing escaping slaves to travel north by following the North Star. Another type of song was the field holler, which has origins in the music of West Africa. It was usually sung in fields when picking cotton or cutting sugar cane and helped give a rhythm to the work.

One area that has preserved much of its original African culture is the sea islands along the coast of North Carolina, South Carolina, Georgia and Florida, home of the Gullah Geechee. One of their traditional musical forms is the Ring Shout. "Shout" does not refer to screaming. Some historians believe it originated from the Arabic word, *saut*, meaning the movement around the Kabaa in Mecca. It uses hand-clapping and foot stomping. Derived from West African traditions, it became a religious practice in the Gullah Geechee culture.

One well-known song evolved from that culture, "Kumbaya." The chorus, "Come By Here," in the Gullah's Creole dialect sounds like cum-by-yah. Over time, pronunciation changed into "Kumbaya." The song is a call to God to come and help the people as they faced oppression. The Gullah Museum in Georgetown, South Carolina is one place to learn more about the music and culture of the Gullah people.

Another place keeping the music and culture alive is Penn Center on St. Helena Island, a museum celebrating the Gullah heritage, it hosts Penn Center's Heritage Days Celebration in November.

Exhibit at the Banjo Museum.

Chapter 4 Cajun and Zydeco

Cajun music is a vital part of Louisiana culture. Their story begins in France when the people who would become the Cajuns left the rural areas of the Vendee region of western France. In 1604, they began settling in what is now Nova Scotia, Canada. It was then known as Acadie. They were mainly farmers and fishermen.

The British began the removal of the Acadians from Canada after England took control of that area of Canada. They herded the Arcadians onto British ships, taking them many places, including Louisiana. It was known in Cajun culture as *Le Grand Dérangement*.

The first group of Acadian exiles were granted asylum in Louisiana in 1755. They settled west of New Orleans, in south-central Louisiana. The Acadians shared the swamps, bayous and prairies with the Attakapa and Chitimacha Native American tribes. Carl Anthony Brasseaux, a Louisiana historian, wrote, "The oldest of the pioneer communities, Fausse Point, was established near present-day Loreauville by late June 1765,"

By the end of the American Revolution, about 1,500 more Acadians arrived in Louisiana. They settled in isolated regions until the early 20th century, so much of the early songs were never written or documented.

"Allons à Lafayette" was the first Cajun song recorded by **Joe Falcon and Cléoma Breaux** in 1928. The song is based on an older traditional tune called "Jeunes gens campagnard." Here are both French and English versions, so you can get a feel for the original Cajun style. Look it up online and play it for the music.

"Jeunes gens campagnard"

Jeunes filles de la campagne
Mariez vous-autres jamais
'Gardez quoi moi j'ai fait
Mis une femme dans l'embarras
Garder c'est pas la peine

Tu essayes à les aimer
Te connais, donc, être musicien
Ça paiera pas comme ça
Jeunes filles de la campagne
Mariez vous-autres jamais
'Gardez quoi moi j'ai fait
Je m'ai mis dans les misères
La femme est malheureuse
Et les enfants est plus
'Gardons comme c'est misérable
Les voir à la traîne comme ça.

English version

Young country girls
Marry yourselves never
'Keep what I've done
Put a woman in trouble
Keeping it's not worth it
You try to love them
Know you, so being a musician
It won't pay like that
I put myself in misery
The woman is unhappy
And the children are more
'Let's keep how miserable it is
to see them left behind like that.

Most Cajun songs are either lively two-steps or waltzes and were written for dancing. Cajun music "belongs" to the Cajun people, but it mingles influences from Irish, German, African, Native American and Appalachian traditions. The Spanish eventually contributed the guitar. The violin, called a fiddle outside of classical circles, was a popular new instrument in France during the 17th century when the French left for the Canada. Acadians used it in Canada by at the time of the expulsion, and it remained the main instrument among Acadian refugees coming to Louisiana. They either brought fiddles with them, or made or purchased one in Louisiana. The fiddle was often the only instrument used at house dances after the Louisiana settlement. Sometimes another simple percussion instrument, the triangle, known in Cajun French as a "tit-fer" or "little iron" was used to provide a strong beat important for dance music.

House dances remained popular into the twentieth century. Since house dances were crowded and noisy, to be heard above the talk and laughter, Cajun fiddlers developed a playing style that bore down hard on bows to play as loud as possible. It gave this music a unique sound.

The dance hall tradition began later. It was called a *Fais do do,* and probably got this name from the practice of bringing children to dance halls to lull them to sleep. In French, *fais do-do* means "go to sleep."

The accordion was accepted on a limited scale by Cajuns by the end of the 19th century. It didn't become popular until the 1920s when accordions were built with keys that were compatible with fiddles.

Bayou Delight in Houma is a great place to visit for a toe-tapping, two-stepping good time. They have a great menu filled with Cajun dishes, but on Friday and Saturdays, it's the music that will draw in the crowds.

Blue Moon in Lafayette is much more rustic and had a hard rocking Zydeco band the night we were there. This place is unique. It features many kinds of music and is strictly a dance hall, not a family restaurant. It is located in the yard and on the back porch of a guesthouse in Lafayette and I doubt the guest do much sleeping on Wednesday through Saturday nights. The joint was really jumping. When I walked in, I just could not keep still. That music really gets to your soul and made you move your feet. It opened in April of 2002 and had been a raging success ever since. In spite of its humble appearance, it has been named in the Top 100 Bars by *Southern Living* and Best Place to Experience Live Music Downtown by the *Downtown Lafayette Association*.

The Acadian Cultural Center is another place in Lafayette to learn about Cajun and Zydeco music and the culture that created this music.

Vermillionville is a living history village about Cajun and Creole culture in Lafayette. Not only can you visit and talk to a local musician about the music, they have many musical events throughout the year.

Harry Choates recorded another old traditional song that is considered the Cajun anthem, and was the first Cajun hit song, "Jolie Blon," in 1946. By then, many other influences crept into Cajun music.

With the discovery of oil in Cajun areas of Louisiana and across the river in Texas, many Cajuns worked with people of African descent in Louisiana, resulted in a merging of musical styles. Black Creoles began playing fiddles and accordions. French-speaking blacks who had been brought over from Haiti learned Cajun songs. The blues infiltrated into Cajun music.

Amédé Ardoin, a Black Creole accordion player, and Dennis McGee, a white Cajun fiddler, crossed racial barriers and defied Jim Crow-era customs to play and record music together as early as 1929. His talent with French music cost Amédé his life. Around 1939, he was severely beaten by two racist white men after a white woman offered him a rag to wipe his face at a dance hall. He was left badly beaten and mentally incapacitated from the attack later that night. Amédé spent the rest of his life in a Louisiana mental hospital and died a few months later. His legacy was that a new style arose, zydeco.

Zydeco is the music of "Creoles of Color" in south Louisiana. Like the Cajuns, the early zydeco music comes from people who spoke French but Creole French rather than the Cajun dialect. The main instruments are also accordion, and guitars, but there won't be a fiddle and there will be a rubboard or frottoir made of corrugated metal worn like a vest and rubbed (originally an old-fashioned washboard was used.) It's one of the few musical instruments native to the United States and was invented and named in 1946 across the Mississippi River in Port Arthur, Texas. Drums which will not be in Cajun bands are often in zydeco. Zydeco has elements of rhythm and blues and pop.

Clifton Chenier, known as the "King of Zydeco," was highly influenced by Ardoin. Chenier was the first to introduce the frottoir. He asked a friend, Willie Landry, a Cajun master welder, to construct a washboard for his brother Cleveland that could be made from a single piece of metal like a vest with shoulder straps resembling a knight's armor.

The name "zydeco" is believed to be a contraction of the song title "Les haricots sont pas salé" meaning "The snap beans are not salty." It comes from the standard practice of using salted pork to season beans. It's a way of saying since the beans are not salty, times are tough since there isn't enough money to buy pork.

If you visit Creole Nature Trail Adventure Point in Sulfur, Louisiana, there is an interactive exhibit explaining the difference between zydeco and Cajun music. You can experiment with the different instruments. Plus, you have the bonus of enjoying up-close views of bayous and marshes and smell the mouth-watering aromas of Cajun cooking. It functions as a visitors center for the Lake Charles area.

If you want to try dancing to zydeco, Buck and Johnny's in Breaux Bridge, Louisiana has a zydeco breakfast every Saturday with a live band. Bayou Teche Brewing in Arnaudville, has a Zydeco Brunch on Sundays.

One festival celebrating Cajun music you do not want to miss is Festivals Acadiens et Créoles held in Lafayette in October.

Zydeco and Cajun instruments at Lake Charles Visitors Center.

AMERICAN MUSIC: BORN IN THE USA

*(Top) D'jalma Garnier, a Creole musician at Vermilionville in Lafayette, LA
(Bottom) Downtown Alive in Lafayette, LA*

*(Top) Band at Lafayette Festivals Acadiens et Créoles
(Bottom) Amis du Teche at Blue Moon*

Chapter 5 Blues

Once upon a time, in the not too distant past, the Mississippi Delta ran on a system where the richest people in the country owned the land and the crops, and the poorest worked the fields to produce the rich man's bounty. In that era, cotton was king. This was where most of those people brought to this country by force lived. The system produced one other important product, American music.

It's the land where the blues were born. It was sired by the songs of slaves in the field, particularly, the Call and Response style heard in the early African Spirituals. The origins of spirituals go back much further than the blues, usually dating back to the middle of the 18th century, when the slaves were Christianized and began to sing and play Christian hymns. The blues were the secular counterpart of spirituals. It was considered the Devil's music played by rural blacks.

From those early beginnings, several styles of music evolved. From blues to the big band sound, it all started here.

The blues were born in the Mississippi Delta in the late 19th century. It was firmly rooted in the alluvial topsoil that the "Father of Waters" spewed across the land when it overflowed its banks, wreaking havoc on anything in its path. After mankind learned to tame the mighty river with levees, they realized the bounty the Mississippi had given them. This land is one of the richest agricultural areas in the world. Almost anything will grow here; cotton, soybeans, corn and vegetables of almost any kind.

Early blues timeline isn't well-defined but believed to be between 1870 and 1900, coinciding with emancipation and the transition from slavery to sharecropping.

The Civil War and 13th amendment might have legally freed African Americans, but economic slavery was still the way of life. The blues were a cry from the soul of men and women who worked the fields from "cain't to cain't" referring to "cain't see in the mornin' 'cause it's too early 'til cain't see at night 'cause it's too late." They had little recourse from the law when they were misused and abused by their employers and any other white men who felt the need to "prove their superiority" at the expense of the lowly cotton pickers or farmworkers. So they poured out their souls in music on the fields and in the ramshackle jook (later evolved into juke as in juke box) joints where they took what pleasures they could at night after their day's labor.

The blues form of the Call and Response with a 12-bar pattern with an AAB format was a common practice in African cultures. AA, the call, is repeated in the first two lines of the song, sometimes with some variation, and B is the response. An example of this format is found in **Bessie Smith**'s song "Down Hearted Blues."

The call is repeated twice "Trouble, trouble I've had it all my days. Trouble, trouble I've had it all my days" then the response in the third line, "It seems like trouble going to follow me to my grave."

Bessie Smith was known as "Empress of the Blues" for the role she played as trailblazer for songs about working class Black women. She along with her reputed sometimes lover, Ma Rainey, openly flaunted her bisexuality. Many of Bessie's songs like "Poor Man's Blues" and "Washwoman's Blues," had a strong resemblance to the protest songs of the 1960s like "Blowing in the Wind" and "R E S P E C T," written by Otis Redding and sung by Aretha Franklin. In 1929, Bessie Smith was cast in the film *St. Louis Blues*, based on. W. C. Handy's song

One of the best-known legends about the blues is the story that **Robert Johnson** sold his soul to the Devil to become a talented blues musician. The story goes that Robert Johnson saw the blues as a way out of the poverty of a subsistence farmer. He became a follower of

Son House, already a legendary Bluesman. Son told Robert Johnson he showed no talent with his guitar playing. Johnson left for a few months, got married, and moved to a farm. When he met see Son House again, he was a fantastic player and no longer had a wife. Son House offered the explanation that Robert Johnson had "sold his sold to the devil at the crossroads" in exchange for his newfound talent.

The legend sites several places where the transaction occurred. The generally accepted spot is the crossroads of Highway 61 and 49. There is a Blues Marker there and a great photo op with the crossroads sign. The Crossroads is sort of the opposite of the "Mother Church of the Blues." You can't miss it, as they marked it with a giant guitar. Ironically, Highway 61 is known as the "Blues Highway" and Highway 49 will lead you to Parchman Prison. Many Bluesmen were familiar with, and have written songs about, that location.

However, that might be too simple. There are many other theories as to the actual crossroads of Robert Johnson's life. I was there with a group of other travel writers, and we visited the Tunica Museum and met Dick Taylor, the executive director. The museum has a lot of exhibits representing the way of life that produced the blues. Director Taylor had his own opinion about the site of the actual crossroads. He stated, "Robert Johnson grew up around here. I was lucky enough to know people who knew him as a child. Wayne Cooper, who worked and grew up with Robert Johnson, said the story is true, but the Crosstown Cemetery is the actual place where Johnson made his deal."

Director Taylor also pointed out that the Devil is reputed to be found near water and this cemetery is right near the Mississippi River at the intersection of Crosstown Road and Bonny Blue Road, not too far from the museum. He told us everyone he sent out there came back with a strange story. They varied from car radios changing to a station the owner had never heard before to car air conditioners quitting. My own experience was my camera battery going dead at that point and repeating the problem at several spots related to Robert Johnson.

Johnson used various aliases and pretty much had a woman in every town to which he traveled. His life was cut short at the age of 27 when he was reputedly poisoned by a jealous husband while playing a juke joint.

Much of his life is obscured by myths. Even his exact burial place is debated. There are three gravestones around the area claiming to be his grave. On a trip to the Delta, I visited one grave that the locals believe is the actual site. There was an eyewitness to Robert Johnson's burial here, one of his former girlfriends. It is located in Little Zion Baptist Church Cemetery.

Gateway to the Blues Museum is located at Tunica Visitors' Center. Any music lover will adore this museum, and it will fascinate even those with only a mild interest. It is filled with artifacts that tell the story of how the blues began. There are lots of guitars tracing the history and evolution of the instrument. It has exhibits with images and instruments for most of the better known Mississippi Delta Bluesmen such as Howlin' Wolf, Muddy Waters, Son House, Robert Johnson, Charlie Patton, Sonny Boy Williamson, Jimmy Reed, one of the few white bluesmen, and many others. You can spend hours there. It's great fun and so enlightening. One of my favorite options this museum offers is a chance to record your own blues song. Go there and record one like I did. Hopefully, you sing better than I do.

Dockery Farms, midway between Clarksdale and Indianola, is the place to visit if you are interested in the typical life of the earlier blues players. Established well after the end of slavery in 1895, it was the home of many of the blues greats. Charlie Patton, Robert Johnson, Howlin' Wolf, Pops Staples, and Honeyboy Edwards all lived and worked at Dockery Farms at one time. This was a typical plantation of the time. It has a marker on the Blues Trail. You can visit and do a self tour or request a guided tour.

The first published blues sheet music is believed to have been "I Got the Blues," published in 1908 by New Orleans musician **Antonio Maggio**. He was a Sicilian who came to New Orleans as a teenager.

He had training in classical music. His official job was a barber, but he spent lots of time playing music in the streets and local bars.

When President McKinley was assassinated, Antonio, known for his socialist and anarchist beliefs, was arrested and held in New Mexico without trial as a suspect. When he was released several months later, he returned to New Orleans. One day, he encountered a Black man on the levee playing a song with just three notes. He was enthralled by the music and asked the man what song he was playing. The man replied, "I got the blues." Antonio immediately began writing a song based on the notes he had heard. He titled it "I got the Blues" and it became an instant hit. Originally, he had not intended to publish it but with the great demand, he published 1000 copies for piano, 500 for band and 500 for orchestra. Interestingly, although it is credited as blues, many places list it as ragtime.

The first recording by an African American singer was **Mamie Smith**'s 1920 rendition of Perry Bradford's "Crazy Blues" on the Okeh label. The recording company received threats from several groups saying they would boycott the company if they recorded a black singer. Her record was a commercial success and opened the door for more black musicians to record.

Another huge influence in the blues was William Christopher Handy, more commonly known as **W. C. Handy**. He is considered the "Father of the Blues." In 1912, when he published "The Memphis Blues," he was already well known as a cornetist and bandleader. The song was originally a campaign song Handy, or possibly his clarinetist, wrote for Edward Crump, the successful Democratic Memphis mayoral candidate in the 1909 election. Handy first published it as an instrumental.

Handy was born in Florence, Alabama in 1873. W. C. Handy Birthplace Museum in Florence is a great place to learn more about his early life. The log cabin where he was born is still owned and operated by his family and contains many of his original photos, music, and documents.

He spent time in Clarksdale, Mississippi when he became interested in the blues. He is credited with taking the blues from a regional music style, Delta blues, to a new level of popularity.

Clarksdale considers itself the epicenter of the blues. It hosts the Juke Joint Festival annually. It has nine Blues Trail Markers, including one for WROX at 257 Delta Avenue, the site of Clarksdale's first African American radio station. WROX featured the famed "King Biscuit Show" and musicians like Ike Turner and Robert Nighthawk. Another place to visit in Clarksdale is the Riverside Hotel, where Bessie Smith died.

The Rock 'n' Blues Museum in Clarksdale has much more of the blues heritage besides the infamous crossroads sign. It is filled to overflowing with memorabilia covering over 50 years of music. Theo Dasbach, museum owner, and himself a musician, fell in love with the blues as a child in Luxemburg, Netherlands. If you want to examine everything in the museum you could be there for days.

Delta Blues Museum in Clarksdale is filled with information and artifacts of the legendary blues musicians and many lesser known ones. For me, the highlight of the museum is the cabin where Muddy Waters lived when he worked as a sharecropper and tractor driver at Stovall Farms. It was on the front steps of this very cabin where Alan Lomax, the ethnomusicologist credited with saving many of the songs of the Delta, recorded Muddy on the front porch for the Library of Congress in 1941. Muddy Waters has markers at the site of the cabin's original location on Stovall Plantation near Clarksdale and at his birthplace in Rolling Fork.

Ground Zero Blues Club was once a cotton-grading warehouse. Downstairs is the club where all walls are covered with intentional graffiti and upstairs are cute retro apartments you can rent for the night or longer.

W. C. Handy moved to Memphis. The W.C. Handy Home and Museum on Beale St. in Memphis features photos, memorabilia, and the desk where he wrote many of his songs. The home was moved to Beale Street in the mid-1980s and restored as an interpretive center operated by Heritage Tours.

In fact, all of Beale Street is a good place to visit to learn about the blues. There is W.C. Handy Park with his stature, and lots of blues music there. After five years on Beale Street in Memphis, Handy moved his music publishing company to the Gaiety Theater Building in New York City. In a letter he wrote in 1949, he claimed that the move made the Handy Brothers Music Company the first Black-owned business on Broadway.

The blues had a "mother" as well. **Ma Rainey,** born Gertrude Pridgett in Columbus, Georgia in 1886, was known as "Mother of the Blues" and released over 100 records with Paramount. She used the name Ma Rainey after her marriage to Will Rainey in 1904. Her career spanned the last years of the 19th and early 20th centuries.

The singers of today who gain attention for their outrageous behaviors have nothing on Ma Rainey. She had many run-ins with the law. One time they arrested her onstage for possession of stolen jewelry. Another time, police raided a house in Chicago where she was staying claiming Rainey was engaging in an orgy with some of her woman band members and charged her with holding an "indecent party." One of her contemporaries, and often reported lover, Bessie Smith, bailed her out the next morning. Bisexual rumors were fueled by Rainey's song, "Prove it on Me," where the poster advertising it had Rainey decked out in a man's hat, suit jacket, vest, and tie talking to two feminine looking women while a policeman looks on in the background.

Her lyrics ran the range from being beaten by "her man" to taking a gun to multiple persons. Her onstage persona usually involved a floor-length dress, her trademark twenty dollar gold pieces necklace and sometimes an outrageous wig. She often held an ostrich plume in one hand and a gun in the other. Her gold teeth would flash as the audience fell captive under her powerful voice that changed from tender to ribald to gutsy from one number to the next.

She recorded over 100 records for Paramount Records and, after they dropped her contract, she continued to perform, but as blues popularity declined, she retired to Columbus. She managed at two theaters in the area but performed at many others.

Ma Rainey's Home in Columbus, Georgia is a good marriage between Ma Rainey, the person, and her musical image with many of her original records and posters from her career. Ma's piano, once painted bright green, now restored, stands in her hall. Deb Wise, our guide, told us about Ma's bedroom set, "her relative sold it to a local antique shop for $200 and we had to pay $15,000 to the shop to get it back when the city restored the house."

Blind Willie McTell was another Georgia blues singer and guitarist. His birthdate is unclear. Some records say May 5, 1898, others say 1903 based on census records. John A. Lomax and his wife, Ruby, interviewed and recorded McTell In 1940 for the *Archive of American Folk Song of the Library of Congress.*

Although McTell was born in Thompson, Georgia, he claimed Statesboro as his home. His most famous song, "Statesboro Blues," has been covered by many modern day singers, including Dolly Parton and the Allman Brothers Band. Statesboro has a statue of him in front of their visitors' center. The small museum in the visitors' center tells about him, as does the Georgia Southern Museum. The new Farmer's market has a beautiful boardwalk leading to the Blind Willie McTell trail that begins at the fairgrounds.

Howlin' Wolf was a good example of the merging of styles. Country singer Jimmie Rodgers was one of his idols. When Howlin' Wolf tried to copy Rodgers's famous yodel, he stated, "I couldn't do no yodelin', so I turned to howlin'. And it's done me just fine."

Howlin' Wolf was born Chester Arthur Burnett on June 10, 1910. He is considered one of the most influential blues musicians of all time and is credited with helping bridge the gap between Delta blues and Chicago blues.

He was also an accomplished harmonica player and credits that to Sonny Boy Williamson II, who taught him how to play in 1933 while he was living in Arkansas. In the 1930s, legendary Delta blues guitarist and singer, Charley Patton, took him under his wing. By the late 1930s, Howlin' Wolf was playing local clubs. Howlin' Wolf got a big break in 1951 when Ike Turner introduced him to Sam Phillips in Memphis at what later became Sun Studio. Phillips was highly impressed, and since Sun Records had not yet been formed, Phillips sponsored Howlin' Wolf's recording at Chess Records where his first single was "Moanin' at Midnight" and "How Many More Years" on the B side. The same year, he recorded "Riding in the Moonlight," "Moaning at Midnight," and "Passing By Blues" "Crying at Daybreak" on Modern's subsidiary RPM Record.

Howlin' Wolf Blues Museum in West Point, Mississippi holds an annual festival in his honor.

Howlin' Wolf's legendary rival was **Muddy Waters**, born McKinley Morganfield in the Mississippi Delta. His birthdate varies but was either 1913 or 1915. He began playing locally on the harmonica and later bought a guitar. After hearing the songs recorded by Alan Lomax, at his home on Stovall Plantation, he moved to Chicago in 1946. He recorded like Howlin' Wolf for Chess Records. Some of his early 1950s songs, including "Hoochie Coochie Man" and "I'm Ready," are considered classic Chicago blues.

The Chicago blues began when many Delta blues singers, as well as other African Americans seeking jobs and escape from harsh Jim Crow Laws, moved to places like Chicago, Saint Louis, and Detroit in the first half of the twentieth century. It's known as the Great Migration. It added electronic instruments and amplifiers to traditional blues and is one of the major influences on early rock and roll.

If one man could be said to have brought the blues to the world's attention, that man is **B. B. King**. His hard work and talent was what raised a young man named Riley B. King from just another Delta sharecropper to the heights of stardom. B. B. King's original dream was simple, "I was going to have me a little farm. I could picture myself plowing, picture seeing a beautiful woman with my two or three kids coming out and bringing me some water. Those were my dreams."

This former sharecropper received 14 Grammys, 2 honorary doctorates, The Presidential Medal of Freedom, the highest civilian award an American can receive, and many other accolades. He met with heads of state, and performed in places he had once only dreamed about. All this to a young man who, when he saw Memphis for the first time said, "Memphis to me then was like the Eiffel Tower, or the Tower of Pisa, or the Grand Canyon. I saw streetcars for the first time. I saw buildings like I had never seen before. God almighty, this was really something."

B. B. King passed away at the age of 89. His music lives on. B. B. King Museum and Delta Interpretive Center, in his hometown of Indianola, Mississippi, chronicles King's life from childhood through his days as a sharecropper and tractor driver to becoming "The King of Blues."

The museum is filed with artifacts B. B. generously donated, clothes, guitars, records, and so much of his personal life. That story begins as you approach the front of the building. You come face to face with a stature of "Lucille" one of his Gibson Guitar. My favorite story there is how his guitar, Lucille, got its name. It came about in Arkansas when he was playing in a rowdy bar. Two men got into a fight and knocked over a barrel of heating oil. It set the bar afire. B. B. escaped but rushed back inside to get his guitar. He named the guitar after the woman the men were fighting over, Lucille, as a reminder never to do such a stupid thing again.

First place to stop in the museum is the theater. It shows a great video of B. B. King's life. Then on to the exhibit of "The Early Years, the Delta 1930s," just inside the museum. It depicts a juke joint and shows scenes of life of a sharecropper in the Delta in the mid-1900s. There are pictures of workers hoeing cotton and little shacks where they lived. The Memphis Gallery depicts the challenges an African American faced in the segregated 50s. One exhibit shows the first radio stations catering to the blues and featuring African American musicians, WGRM and WROX. It was in Memphis that he gained the name "B. B." standing for Blues Boy. The exhibits take you through his first break, recording "Three O'clock Blues" and going on the road in a country that still had a big color line. He played what was known as the "Chitlin' Circuit." He worked not only to gain popularity for his own songs but to gain respect and a wider audience for the blues. By the 60s, B. B. King was a respected name.

The museum exhibits portray the awakening Civil Right Movement and the effect it had on the blues. The later year exhibits portray the honors heaped on this former sharecropper. King has received 14 Grammys, two honorary doctorates, the highest civilian award an American can receive, The Presidential Medal of Freedom, and many other accolades He met with heads of state and performed in places he had once only dreamed about. There is a "Recording Studio" where you can try your hand at you own style of the blues. It's a place you do not want to miss.

The King of Blues is buried just outside the museum. There is a memorial courtyard around his grave with a life-size bronze of King holding his beloved Lucille created by sculptor Toby Mendez.

The portion of Highway 61 that runs from St. Louis, Missouri to Memphis, Tennessee, through the Mississippi Delta, and on to New Orleans is known as "The Blues Highway." The state of Mississippi has created a Blues Trail with over 150 markers and growing to honor those who contributed to the birth of the blues. (They have a County Music Trail that often overlaps.)

As you drive into Mississippi from Memphis, you soon find the markers. The marker on the corner of Second and Church Street in Indianola, where B. B. King would hang out and play for tips as a teenager, is sort of the grandfather of the Mississippi Blues Trail. It, along with a sister marker at Club Ebony, later replaced by the "official" Blues Trail Marker, was done as an effort to convince the state of Mississippi to move forward with a Blues Trail project. Besides the marker, B. B. King embedded his handprints and engraved his name into the cement. There is also an image of his guitar, Lucille, and a portrait of young Riley B. King before he went to Memphis and acquired the name he is known worldwide by today, B. B. King. This marker was placed in June 2003, well before the first official marker for the Mississippi Blues Trail was installed on December 11, 2006. You will notice this marker is slightly different from the others and refers to a "Mississippi Delta Blues Trail" that the project was originally conceived to be.

One important blues stop in DeSoto County in the town of Hernando is the DeSoto County Museum. View the exhibit on Miss Mary Cotton's Café, considered the most famous juke joint in DeSoto County. Blues musicians, including Robert Wilkins, Jim Jackson, Gus Cannon, and Memphis Minnie, played there. Memphis Minnie's and Joe Callicott's graves and trail markers on the Mississippi Blues Trail, along with The Dickinson Family, are nearby.

The county's most famous resident associated with a later evolution of music is Jerry Lee Lewis. The museum displays one of his pianos.

100 Men Hall in Bay St. Louis, Mississippi was a hotspot on the Chitlin' circuit back in the days of segregation. Musicians would come to play there. After their show, they could come by the depot and hop aboard the next freight train headed for New Orleans or their next gig. 100 Men Hall has been beautifully remodeled and now hosts events, celebrations of all different cultures.

John Lee Hooker represents the crossover when many of the delta Mississippi African Americans moved to Detroit for the available factory jobs. He began life in either Tutwiler or near Clarksdale, Mississippi. His birthdate is cloudy ranging from possibly 1912 to 1917. Growing up the son of a Baptist preacher, his earliest influence was spirituals. He never heard blues until 1922 when his mother, Minnie, who had divorced his father the previous year, married William Moore, a blues singer who played in Shreveport, Louisiana. Moore introduced young John Lee to the guitar and taught him the fundamentals of what became Hooker's traditional style, a driving-rhythm boogie beat.

As a teen he ran away from home and played in Memphis awhile, then drifted around and settled in Detroit. His first single, "Boogie Chillen'," recorded for Modern Records became a hit and the best-selling "race record" in 1949. When he played in noisy Detroit clubs, he changed to an electric guitar. In his later years he played with rock bands. Two of his songs, "Boogie Chillen" and "Boom Boom," are included in the Rock and Roll Hall of Fame's list of the 500 Songs That Shaped Rock and Roll.

"Sleepy" John Estes, early bluesman at the West Tennessee Delta Heritage Museum in Brownsville, TN

(Top) Ma Rainey's bedroom in Columbus, Georgia
(Bottom) Tunica Visitors Center/Museum

Crossroads where Robert Johnson allegedly sold his soul to the devil

(top) Ground Zero Blues Club in Clarksdale, MS
(bottom) An exhibit from B.B. King Museum in Indianola, MS

B. B. King's guitar, Lucille, in front of his museum

*(Top)One of the blues exhibits at DeSoto Museum
(Bottom) Exhibit at St. Louis Blues Museum*

Chapter 6 Ragtime

The popular style of American music from about 1899 to 1917 was ragtime. Ragtime began with honky-tonk pianists along the Mississippi and Missouri rivers. Ragtime originally was formally structured piano compositions, but there were banjo versions and it had touches of the minstrel-show songs, African American banjo songs, and influences from old European music. It was formally structured piano compositions considered by the composers to be classical music. It was not originally meant for dancing but as bands picked up the songs it became a style of dance music. The word ragtime is probably a contraction of "ragged-time" denoting a ragged kind of piano music. Time was commonly used to denote music style then such as Waltz-time or March-time.

St. Louis, Missouri and New Orleans were the main hotspots. **Scott Joplin** is considered the "King of Ragtime." He was born in Texas and spend much of his early year in Texarkana. Unsubstantiated stories say as a child, Scott was given access to a piano in a white-owned home where his mother worked. With it, he taught himself the basics.

A German-born Jewish music professor, Julius Weiss, who immigrated to Texas in the late 1860s and taught music to the children of prominent local families, was impressed by Scott's talent. He tutored Scott free of charge from the ages of 11 to 16 and introduced him to folk and classical music.

Scott Joplin traveled to Chicago in 1893 to play his music at clubs and brothels around the World Fair. As an adult, he made his home in Sedalia, Missouri, where he wrote one of his most successful rags, "The Maple Leaf Rag," in 1899.

The publisher was John Stark, a Civil War veteran who had come to Sedalia in 1886. He first opened a music store and later began publishing. Stark and Scott met in 1899. When Scott came to Stark's store and showed him "Maple Leaf Rag," Stark was impressed. Joplin moved to St. Louis in 1901. Stark also moved his publishing company there.

In 1913 Scott, with his new wife Lottie, started his own publishing company, and published "Magnetic Rag" in 1914. During his lifetime, he wrote over 40 original ragtime pieces, one ragtime ballet, and two operas none of the latter were published and the manuscripts have been lost. He died of complications from syphilis on April 1, 1917.

A visit to the Katy Depot Museum in Sedalia, MO, also the city's welcome center, is a good starting place to learn his story. The old depot, turned museum, tells about Scott Joplin's time in Sedalia when he wrote his early songs. Out back on the railroad tracks, you can see the beautiful blue "Syncopated Rhythm Piano" created by John Guffin in 2004. There is also a great mural of him in the historic district. Sedalia holds an annual Scott Joplin Ragtime Festival the first weekend in June and offers a walking tour of places significant in his life.

Move on to St. Louis and visit the home where Scott Joplin boarded and wrote many of his ragtime hits. Our guide even "played" one of his rags on his player piano.

While in St. Louis, Scott associated with another popular ragtime pioneer and saloon owner, **Thomas M. Turpin** considered the Father of St. Louis Ragtime. Turpin was originally from Savannah, Georgia. His father, John Turpin, was politically active during Reconstruction and was called "Honest John." In the early 1880s, John moved to St. Louis and opened the Silver Dollar Saloon. It was torn down in 1903 to build a railroad station in anticipation of the St. Louis Exposition of 1904. Tom Turpin published his "Harlem Rag" in 1897. It was the first published instrumental rag by an African American composer.

Turpin only published four other rags in his lifetime; "The Bowery Buck" in 1899, "A Ragtime Nightmare" in 1900, "St. Louis Rag" in

1903, and "The Buffalo Rag" in 1904. His influence was mainly because of his salon, The Rosebud café. It was a regular stomping ground for St. Louis' best rag players and an almost mandatory stop for any musician traveling through St. Louis. Tom Turpin died in 1922.

Another Midwest ragtime composer was **Ernest Hogan.** His songs were among the first ragtime songs to get published and were the first to use the word "rag" on the sheet music. He was born Ernest Reuben Crowdus in 1865 in Kentucky's Shake Rag District of Bowling Green. His career began early. He worked in traveling minstrel shows as a dancer, musician, and comedian while in his teens.

In 1895, he wrote several popular songs, one of which has ugly connotations. "All Coons Look Alike to Me" has a Black man's girlfriend telling him why she threw him over for another Black man who had more money. Its use of a racial slur and stereotype created many derogatory imitations, known as "coon songs." Ernest Hogan adapted some of the song from one he heard in Chicago called "All Pimps Look Alike to Me."

Although he was considered one of the most talented performers of his time, his heritage is a mixed bag because of such a racial slur in a song written by a Black man. Before his death he appeared to regret his composition, yet explained it as having a good side. He commented, "That song caused a lot of trouble in and out of show business, but it was also good for show business because at the time, money was short in all walks of life. With the publication of that song, a new musical rhythm was given to the people. Its popularity grew and, it sold like wildfire... That one song opened the way for a lot of colored and white songwriters. Finding the rhythm so great, they stuck to it ... and now you get hit songs without the word 'coon.' Ragtime was the rhythm played in backrooms and cafes and such places. The ragtime players were the boys who played just by ear their own creations of music which would have been lost to the world if I had not put it on paper."

Some of his other works include "La Pas Ma La" and "The Missionary Man." He died of tuberculous in 1909.

Antonio Junius **"Tony" Jackson** was born to poor African American parents in Uptown New Orleans in 1882. He has epilepsy from birth but was a child prodigy. By the age of 10, he built a working and well-tuned harpsichord out of junk because his family could not afford a piano. He would play hymns he heard in church from memory. He got his first musical gig around the age of 13 when he began playing piano in a Storyville joint. (For those not familiar with New Orleans history, Storyville was a semi-legal district where prostitution was allowed. It was named for conservative City Alderman, Sidney Story, who set the district up, but was not happy with the nomenclature.) Of course Jackson used the prefix, "professor," as did other piano players there. They were the highest-ranking musicians, thus "professor." By fifteen, he was considered one of the best pianists in that part of New Orleans. He was able to remember and play any tune he had heard once from ragtime, cakewalks, Broadway, or other genre. One of his gimmicks was to dance a high kicking cakewalk while playing his piano.

He was openly homosexual and eventually moved to Chicago, where homosexuality was more accepted. There were few songs published with Tony Jackson's name on them, as he either sold the rights, or had his music compositions stolen from him. "Pretty Baby" is his most famous composition. Tony became a mentor to Jelly Roll Morton, whom you'll hear more about in the Jazz chapter. He died in 1921. In 2011, he was inducted into the Chicago Gay and Lesbian Hall of Fame.

Our guide at Scott Joplin House "playing" a rag on Joplin's player piano

Chapter 7 Jazz

Ragtime was a direct precursor to jazz. Jazz was born in New Orleans when Buddy Bolden began improvising with the music he played in the Storyville brothels.

Born Charles Joseph **"Buddy" Bolden** on September 6, 1877, in New Orleans, Bolden is considered the "Father of Jazz." He was an African American cornetist who began played the music he heard by ear and improvising it for his horn. This was an exciting fusion of ragtime, Black gospel music, marching-band music, and Southern blues. He rearranged his New Orleans dance band to better accommodate this combination of music. The string instruments became the rhythm section, clarinets, trombones, and Bolden's cornet as front line instruments.

One of his composition is "Funky Butt" which came to be known as "Buddy Bolden's Blues." another jazz musician, Danny Barker, described it as a reference to the olfactory effect of an auditorium packed full of sweaty people "dancing close together and belly rubbing."

Buddy Bolden married Hattie Oliver, and they had one child named Charles Joseph Bolden, Jr. Buddy's great-grandson, Sammie "Big Sam" Williams, is a local New Orleans musician.

Buddy was an alcoholic and developed what is known today as schizophrenia. He was institutionalized at the Louisiana State Insane Asylum at Jackson in 1907 until his death on November 4, 1931.

Jelly Roll Morton was born Ferdinand Joseph LaMothe around 1890 into the Creole community of the Faubourg Marigny neighborhood in New Orleans. No birth certificate was issued for him, as the law requiring birth certificates for citizens was not enforced until 1914. He claimed different dates in his lifetime. At the age of fourteen, Jelly Roll began playing piano in a Storyville brothel. His family were Catholics and looked down on professional musicians, so he used the nickname "Jelly Roll," common African American slang of the time for female genitalia, and Morton, an anglicized version of his stepfather, William Mouton's name to keep his family from finding out he was a brothel "professor."

Jelly Roll started touring in the South with his girlfriend, Rosa Brown, playing in minstrel shows around 1904. He began writing music around this time composing "Jelly Roll Blues," "New Orleans Blues," "Frog-I-More Rag," "Animule Dance," and "King Porter Stomp." His "Jelly Roll Blues," published in 1915, was one of the first published jazz compositions.

He lived in Chicago for three years. By 1914, he was putting his compositions on paper. In 1926, he signed a contract with the Victor Talking Machine Company, letting him bring his own band, the Red Hot Peppers composed of Kid Ory, Johnny St. Cyr, George Mitchell, Barney Bigard, Omer Simeon, Johnny Dodds, Baby Dodds, and Andrew Hilaire, to play his arrangements in their recording studios in Chicago.

Jelly Roll moved first to New York City, where he continued to record for Victor. Then in 1935, he moved to Washington, D.C., to manage and play piano at a bar called the Music Box, and later Blue Moon Inn, and Jungle Inn. In 1938, a friend of the Music Box's owner stabbed him in the head and chest. The nearest whites-only hospital refused to treat him because of segregation. He was then sent to a black hospital farther away. The doctors there failed to treat the wound effectively, causing him to develop severe asthma problems. He lived for a time in New York and Los Angeles, where died on July 10, 1941.

New Orleans most famous jazz musician was **Louis Armstrong**. His 1939 recording of "When the Saints Go Marchin in" is in large part the reason for the New Orleans football team's name, The Saints. Louis Daniel Armstrong has been known as "Satchmo," "Satch," and "Pops," but the world remembers him as Louis Armstrong, (pronounced "Louie.") He was born August 4, 1901, and raised in a rough neighborhood on Rampart Street just above Canal Street in New Orleans. Raised by a young single mother, by the age of six, he worked for the Karnoffskys, a family of Lithuanian Jews, who employed his mother. He would help their two sons, Morris and Alex, on what was known as a rag cart. In the 1950s and early '60s, the ragman was a common sight. I remember them riding through the streets in a horse and wagon, usually in less affluent neighborhoods like the Ninth Ward, and call out "Bring me your old clothes and rags."

Young Louis used his musical talents to improve the rag business. He would play a tin horn to attract customers. The boys' father, Morris Karnoffsky, treated Armstrong like a son and gave him money to buy his first coronet. It was here he saw discrimination practiced against other white people similar to how his own race was treated. In their honor, Armstrong wore a Star of David until the end of his life.

By age eleven, Louis dropped out of school and ran with some other street boys who sang for money. He was nicknamed "Satchel Mouth" and later shortened to "Satchmo" because friends said his mouth looked like a satchel. He soon got into trouble for firing a gun loaded with a blank to celebrate New Year's Eve and was arrested on December 31, 1912. He was sent to the Colored Waif's Home, a strict and spartan facility run by Captain Joseph Jones. Louis did have one benefit at the home. Captain Jones had Peter Davis, a popular music teacher in New Orleans, appointed Director of Music at the home. Davis became Louis's first teacher, and recognizing the boy's talent, made him the bandleader. While playing with this band, thirteen-year-old Louis attracted the attention of Kid Ory, who played in Jelly Roll Morton's band, Red Hot Peppers.

While still in his teens, Louis played in brass bands on the riverboats in New Orleans. By twenty, he could read music. He was one of the first jazz musicians to play extended trumpet solos, which he did with his specific style. He began doing vocals too. While performing at the Brick House in Gretna, Louisiana, he met Daisy Parker, a local prostitute, whom he married in 1919. They separated in 1923.

In 1922, he moved to Chicago and played second cornet in King Oliver's Creole Jazz Band. Louis would return to New Orleans off and on all his life. He made his first studio recordings with Oliver for Gennett Records in 1923. He and Oliver parted amicably in 1924, partly at the urging of Lil Hardin Armstrong, King Oliver's pianist whom Armstrong married on February 4, 1924. They moved to New York City to play with the Fletcher Henderson Orchestra, the top African-American band of that time. He switched to the trumpet which blended better with the other band musicians. Armstrong and Hunter divorced in 1931. He then married Alpha Smith, who he met while playing at the Vendome in the

1920s. This marriage ended in 1942. His last marriage was October 1942 to Lucille Wilson, a singer at the Cotton Club in New York.

Over the years Louis Armstrong recorded with some of the most prominent singers of his time, including Bing Crosby, Duke Ellington, Ma Rainey, Bessie Smith, Fletcher Henderson, Earl Hines, Jimmie Rodgers, and Ella Fitzgerald. He and Fitzgerald recorded two albums together; "Ella and Louis" and "Ella and Louis Again." He did two recordings for Columbia Records, "Louis Armstrong Plays W.C. Handy" in 1954, and "Satch Plays Fats," a collection of Fats Waller tunes, in 1955.

Louis was equally gifted as a composer and wrote over fifty songs including "Gully Low Blues," "Potato Head Blues," "Hear Me Talkin' to Ya," "Weather Bird Rag," and "Swing That Music."

Nineteen of his records ranked in the Top Ten and become classics like "Stardust," "What a Wonderful World," "When The Saints Go Marching In," and "Ain't Misbehavin'." His version of "We Have All the Time in the World" was the soundtrack of the James Bond film *On Her Majesty's Secret Service* and his 1964 song "'Bout Time" was featured in the 2005 film *Bewitched*.

His "Hello, Dolly" shoved The Beatles off the top of the Billboard Hot 100 chart in 1964. It also set the US record as the oldest artist to have a number one song. He was 63-year-old.

Louis Armstrong covered so many genres, it's a shame to just call him a jazz musician. He was on Johnny Cash Show on October 28, 1970, and covered Nat King Cole's hit "Ramblin' Rose." He then recreated his performance backing Jimmie Rodgers on "Blue Yodel No. 9." A fantastic mix of Jimmie Roger's country and Armstrong's jazz with piano blues in the mix. Proof of how beautifully American music merges.

In 1969, he played the bandleader, Louis, and sang "Hello Dolly!" with Barbra Streisand in Gene Kelly's film version of *Hello, Dolly!*.

Louis Armstrong died of a heart attack in his sleep on July 6, 1971, in Queens, New York. Louis Armstrong has received more well-deserved honors than almost any other musician.

His recordings were inducted into the Grammy Hall of Fame, and he was posthumously awarded the Grammy Lifetime Achievement Award in 1972 by the Academy of Recording Arts and Sciences.

The Rock and Roll Hall of Fame listed his "West End Blues" on the list of 500 songs that shaped Rock and Roll. In 1999, he was nominated for inclusion in the American Film Institute's 100 Years 100 Stars. The Louis Armstrong's Hot Five and Hot Seven recordings from 1925 to 1928 were preserved in 2002, in the US National Recording Registry. The US Open tennis tournament's former main stadium was renamed Louis Armstrong Stadium. Armstrong had lived a few blocks from the stadium. He was honored with the Louis Armstrong 32-cent commemorative postage stamp In 1995. There is even an asteroid, 9179 Satchmo, named in his honor in 1991.

His former home in Queens, New York was declared a National Historic Landmark in 1977 and is now a museum, The Louis Armstrong House Museum. They offer concerts and educational programs, along with the house museum.

In the summer of 2001, New Orleans's airport was renamed Louis Armstrong New Orleans International Airport to commemorate the centennial of Armstrong's birth. A statue of Armstrong playing his cornet stands at the entrance to the airport's former terminal building.

Congo Square was a common gathering place for African-Americans in New Orleans in the 1800s for dancing and music. (See more about this in Chapter 2.) The park where Congo Square is located was renamed Louis Armstrong Park. It has monuments including a 12-foot statue of Louis Armstrong, a bust of Sidney Bechet, and a depiction of Buddy Bolden. It is the home of many events, including the "Jazz in the Park," a free concert series, and the Louisiana Cajun & Zydeco Festival. The auditorium there is now named Louis Armstrong Auditorium.

New Orleans Jazz Museum occupies the second floor of the Old Mint, and has the world's largest collection of Jazz instruments. There are exhibits about Jazz legends like Bix Beiderbecke, George Lewis, Edward "Kid" Ory, Sidney Bechet, and Dizzy Gillespie. Louis Armstrong's cornet and Fats Domino's piano are the highlights for me. I'm a big fan of both. It hosts annual festivals, including the annual Satchmo Fest. It is a great place to get a feel for New Orleans' early Jazz. Preservation Hall is another good place to hear real jazz.

The biggest jazz fest of all is The New Orleans Jazz & Heritage Festival held annually at the racetrack. It brings in some of the biggest names in the music industry and draws thousands of visitors. No jazz lover should miss it.

Baker's Keyboard Lounge in Detroit claims to be the oldest continuously operated jazz club in the world. I loved clowning around on the same stage where Louis Armstrong, Ella Fitzgerald, Fats Waller, Nat King Cole, Aretha Franklin and most of the biggest jazz names played. Baker's opened May 1934 as a diner, but the owner's son, Clarence Baker, added a piano and some jazz music. The first thing you notice in Baker's is their bar. It's a giant piano, minus playability but with plenty of charm. They have live music.

Statue of Louis Armstrong at Louis Armstrong Park in New Orleans

*(Top) Author and friends clowning around at Baker's Lounge in Detroit
(Bottom) Satchmo Festival in New Orleans*

Chapter 8 Bebop

During WWII, big band or swing jazz began to evolve into a newer style called bebop. Many musicians were now in the military so smaller bands began to take front and center.

Charlie Parker was a leading figure in the development of bebop. His life is both tragic and inspirational. He Was born in Kansas City, Kansas, in 1920. The American Museum of Jazz in Kansas City, Missouri features Charlie Parker as one of the four featured musicians along with Louis Armstrong, Ella Fitzgerald, and Duke Ellington. The museum has a mixing room where visitors can mix their own versions. Their Blue Room is where you can listen to top jazz musicians play.

Charlie began playing the saxophone at age 11. By 14 he was playing in his school band. After his father left, his mother worked nights and young Parker was free to roam Kansas City streets. He dropped out of school. Not unexpectedly he found alcohol and drugs at the same time he was polishing his musical skills. He married his childhood sweetheart, Rebecca Ruffin, on July 25, 1936 when they were both just 16.

In the fall of that year his life took a tragic turn. While traveling with a band to play a gig for the opening of Clarence Musser's Tavern south of Eldon, Missouri the car he was in collided with another vehicle. He suffered three broken ribs and a fractured spine. Doctors weren't sure he would ever walk again. The accident led to Parker's heavy use of painkillers and opioids, especially heroin, which became a lifelong addiction along with alcohol.

By the next year, he was walking and playing music again. He toured with McShann's band in the southwest, Chicago, and New York City. He made his first professional recording debut with McShann's band.

It was as the result of an incident on a tour bus with other musicians that he acquired the nickname, "Yardbird," often shortened to "Bird." While the bus was going down the road, a chicken wandered out in the middle of the road and got hit. Parker had the driver stop. He went out and picked up the dead bird, which he later plucked and cooked for dinner that night.

By 1939, his marriage ended, and he moved to New York City. It was here he achieved the breakthrough that revolutionized jazz. He was experimenting with the song "Cherokee" during a practice session when he hit upon a new method for developing his solos.

It was in 1939 in New York that Bird had the musical breakthrough that had begun in 1937 in the Missouri Ozarks. Playing through the changes, he discovered a new musical vocabulary and sound that shifted the course of music history. Much as I love music, I'm lost with the technical aspect so, I'll give you Charlie Parker's own words. "I was jamming in a chili house on Seventh Avenue between 139th and 140th. It was December 1939. Now I'd been getting bored with the stereotyped changes that were being used all the time at the time, and I kept thinking there's bound to be something else. I could hear it sometimes but I couldn't play it ... Well, that night I was working over 'Cherokee' and, as I did, I found that by using the higher intervals of a chord as a melody line and backing them with appropriately related changes, I could play the thing I'd been hearing. I came alive."

In 1942 he left McShann's band and played for a year with Earl Hines, where he worked with another jazz legend, Dizzy Gillespie.

Because of the two-year Musicians' Union strike which banned all commercial recordings from 1942 to 1944, much of bebop's early development was not recorded or well known. Parker and other early beboppers used smaller groups, improvisations, and shifted to uncharted solos.

The collaboration between Charlie Parker and Dizzy Gillespie created some of the first original recordings of bebop included the historic bebop song "Groovin' High."

During the mid-'40s, he traveled to the West Coast, and played in Los Angeles with trumpeter Miles Davis. In July 1946, he recorded one of his most famous pieces "Lover Man." "Koko," which is his bebop rendition based on "Cherokee," is another classic. In 1953, he recorded "Charlie Parker with Strings and Jazz at Massey Hall".

While his musical career was ascending, his personal life was coming apart. He had two other short-lived marriages and several bouts with mental illness. Shortly after recording "Lover Man," he had a breakdown. He ran naked around Parker's hotel lobby where he was staying and then set the mattress in his room on fire. Police and firemen were called, and he was jailed and admitted to Camarillo State Hospital for six months. With the loss of his young daughter from his common-law-marriage to Chan Woods, he fell deeper into depression. He attempted suicide twice in 1954, resulting in another mental hospital commitment.

He died of lobar pneumonia on March 12, 1955. At his death, he also had an advanced case of cirrhosis and had suffered a heart attack. The coroner performing his autopsy estimated the body to be between 50 and 60 years of age. Charlie Parker was 34-years-old.

Several of his recordings were inducted into the Grammy Hall of Fame, which is a special Grammy Award established in 1973 to honor recordings that are at least twenty-five years old, and that have "qualitative or historical significance."

In 2002, the Library of Congress honored his recording "Ko-Ko" by adding it to the National Recording Registry. In 1995, the U.S. Postal Service issued a 32-cent commemorative postage stamp in Parker's honor.

He is buried in a cemetery in KC. Jazz lovers visit to honor him.
Charlie Parker has long been celebrated by artists, writers, and musicians. Located in the heart of 18th and Vine near the American Jazz Museum, the 10' bronze sculpture by **Robert Graham** celebrates the enduring legacy of Charlie Parker. Charlie's daughter Kim and his third wife Doris attended the 1999 dedication of the statue, which was funded by the Jules and Doris Stein and Oppenheimer Brothers Foundations.

Thelonious Sphere Monk was an American jazz pianist born in Rocky Mount, North Carolina in 1917. His family moved to Manhattan, New York City in 1922, to a neighborhood known as San Juan Hill because of the many African American veterans of the Spanish–American War who lived there.

Monk took piano lessons from a neighbor, Alberta Simmons, starting at six years old. She taught him stride style playing which is a style of jazz piano playing where the right hand plays the melody while the left hand alternates between a single note and a chord played an octave or higher. He learned some hymns, and would sometimes accompany his mother's singing at church. He started learning the classics, but his main focus was jazz music.

He attended a public school for gifted students, but didn't graduate. At 17, he toured with an evangelist, playing the church organ. He began to find work playing jazz as the house pianist at Minton's Playhouse, a Manhattan nightclub and participated in after-hours cutting contests where he honed his skills. Cutting contest are competitions where musicians compete against one another. Monk's style helped form bebop. Some jazz historians refer to him as "the high priest of bebop." He dressed the part wearing a goatee, dark sunglasses and exotic hats. He had a habit of patting his feet while he was playing. Often another band member was playing solo, he would get up and danced around, then return and begin playing. He composed what is called the bebop anthem, "52nd Street Theme."

Monk made his first recordings for Blue Note between 1947 and 1952 where he composed original pieces, he then signed a contract With Prestige Records for the following two years. Riverside bought his Prestige contract for a mere $108.24. Although he was highly regarded by his peers, his records didn't sell. He recorded two albums of jazz standards as a means of improving his standing; "Thelonious Monk Plays Duke Ellington" in 1955 and "The Unique Thelonious Monk" in 1956. On "Brilliant Corners," recorded in late 1956, Monk mainly performed his own music. This album is regarded as the first commercial success for Monk. "Crepuscule with Nellie," that he recorded in 1957, was Monk's only, composition where there is no improvising.

Monk married Nellie Smith in 1947, they had a daughter who died in 1984, and a son, T. S. Monk nicknamed Toot, who is a jazz drummer.

Throughout his career, Monk had several drug possession charges. His first was in August 1951, when New York City police searched a parked car occupied by Monk and a friend Bud Powell. They found narcotics in the car, supposedly belonging to Powell. Monk refused to testify and lost his New York City Cabaret Card. Without this, Monk was legally unable to play in any New York venue where liquor was served. This limited his ability to perform for several years until he discovered some Black-owned bars and clubs in Brooklyn that ignored the law. This gave him smaller little-advertised, one-night engagements. Monk spent most of the early and mid-1950s composing and performing at theaters, events that didn't serve alcohol, and out-of-town venues. In 1954, Monk paid his first visit to Paris where he performed concerts and recorded a solo piano session for French radio.

When he got his cabaret card restored in June 1957, Monk relaunched his New York career in the East Village with a six-month residency at the Five Spot Café. He led a quartet with John Coltrane on tenor saxophone, Wilbur Ware on bass, and Shadow Wilson on drums. That engagement ended Christmas 1957 and the group split up. Monk formed another band in June 1958 when he began a second residency at the Five Spot. This group had Griffin first and later, Charlie Rouse, on tenor, Ahmed Abdul-Malik on bass, and Roy Haynes on drums.

On October 15, 1958, he had another drug related run in with police. This time in Wilmington, Delaware while driving to an engagement with his friend, Baroness Pannonica "Nica" de Koenigswarter, a member of the Rothschild family and a patroness of several New York City jazz musicians. Monk refused to cooperate with the policemen, and they beat him with a blackjack. Even though the police had authorization to search the vehicle and found narcotics, Judge Christie of the Delaware Superior Court ruled that the detention of the pair, unlawful because of the beating of Monk, which rendered the consent to the search void since it was given under duress.

Monk signed in 1962 with Columbia Records, his first Columbia album, "Monk's Dream," was released in 1963. It became his best-selling LP and on February 28, 1964, he was featured on the cover of *Time* magazine in the article "The Loneliest Monk." His next album was "Criss Cross" also in 1963, and "Underground," in 1968. His last studio recordings were made in November 1971 for the English Black Lion label,

Monk was making few appearances by the mid-1970s for health reasons The documentary film *Thelonious Monk: Straight, No*

Chaser filmed in 1988 attributes Monk's strange behavior to mental illness. In the documentary, Monk's son, Toot, says that his father sometimes did not recognize him. Monk was hospitalized several times for mental illness that worsened in the late 1960s. He died of a stroke on February 17, 1982.

Cheraw, South Carolina is noted for many things but for music fans one stands out. It's the home of **Dizzy Gillespie**. John Birks Gillespie was born here on October 21, 1917. His childhood had a few bumps in the road. His father, who was a bricklayer and part-time musician, died when Gillespie was only ten.

Around the time of his father's death, Dizzy's English teacher, perhaps trying to fill a need for the child, introduced him to music. It was love at first note. Dizzy joined the school band, first playing the trombone, but found his real calling and switched to the trumpet. This small step in his education put him on his life's path. He soon earned a scholarship to Laurinberg Institute in North Carolina. Dizzy Gillespie went on to become one of the biggest names in the jazz world and a major founder of BeBop Music.

As a teen, he earned the nickname "Dizzy" for his quirky behavior both off and on stage. One instance was when he began carrying his new trumpet in a paper bag while playing with the Frankie Fairfax band in Philadelphia.

He began playing for both Black and white audiences in Cheraw very young. His family moved to Philadelphia in the early 1930s. He never forgot where he came from and often opened his shows with, "I'm Dizzy Gillespie from Cheraw, South Carolina."

An incident that happened in 1953 helped shape his sound and his image. Someone accidentally fell on top of his trumpet and bent it. When he played the bent instrument, Gillespie found he liked the clearer sound and so had new instruments made with a similar bend for then on. The dented trumpet and his naturally puffy cheeks became his trademark.

He moved to New York around age nineteen and played with such household names as Cab Calloway, Charley Parker, Duke Ellington, Sarah Vaughn, Ella Fitzgerald and others.

He loved to play a unique solo style with his trumpet, but it wasn't until he formed his own band, and began playing at the Onyx Club on 52nd Street that he was free to perform his own music. He performed often with Charlie Parker, and they previewed the "Big Bang" of jazz. In his book, *To Be or Not to Bop*, Gillespie stated, "The opening of the Onyx Club represented the birth of the bebop era."

In 1990, Dizzy Gillespie was awarded the National Medal of the Arts by President Bush. He received a Grammy Award for Best Improvised Jazz in 1976, Grammy Lifetime Achievement Award in 1989, Grammy Award for Best Large Jazz Ensemble Album in 1992. In 1995, he was inducted into the Grammy Hall of Fame. He received the Paul Robeson Award from Rutgers University Institute of Jazz Studies in 1972, Duke Ellington Award from the society of Composers, Authors, and Publishers in 1989 and Kennedy Center for Honors Award in 1990. Posthumously, in 1998, he received the Porin Award for Best Foreign Jazz Music Album. He died January 6, 1993.

Dizzy Gillespie Park was built on the site of his childhood home in Cheraw. There's a South Carolina Historic Marker honoring Gillespie there. You can sit on the stainless steel benches and contemplate the sculptures designed by artist Bob Doster collaborating with Cheraw school children. Doster's stainless steel fence contains the notes of "Salt Peanuts," one of Gillespie's best known works.

The Town Green displays a 7-foot bronze statue, designed by renowned artist Ed Dwight, of Gillespie playing his famous misshapen trumpet At the base inscriptions highlight his career.

Across the street visit the Theater on the Green where Gillespie enjoyed watching movies as a boy. He often snuck in until the theater found a unique solution. They hired him as a "bouncer" to keep other kids from sneaking in and paid him with free admission.

One of the well known jazz and Dixieland performers on Bourbon in the 1950s included Louis Prima, who led the band at the Sho Bar for a time, and Pete Fountain, who played at a number of clubs for much of the decade.

Top) Dizzy Gillespie Park in Cheraw, SC (Bottom) American Jazz Museum Kansas City

Chapter 9 Women in Jazz

Women are sadly under represented in jazz as they were in country music. *Downbeat*, founded in Chicago in 1934 and one of the most popular magazines dedicated to jazz and blues, reported this in their February 11, 1941. Marvin Freedman, writing a critique under the heading "Philosophy and Stuff," stated that women do not like jazz because, "Good jazz is hard masculine music with a whip to it. Women like violins, and jazz deals with drums and trumpets."

This was a typical attitude during the jazz age. In spite of this, women played a role in jazz in all its forms. Usually women in jazz were the singers, but one group made musical history as a band. The **International Sweethearts of Rhythm** was the first integrated all women's band in the United States. The Sweethearts began in the rural junction of Piney Woods, Miss., in 1937. They were originally the Piney Woods Country Life School in Mississippi for poor and African American children's school band.

Dr. Laurence Clifton Jones, the school's principal and founder, began the band to raise money for the school. He picked the name International Sweethearts of Rhythm because there were girls of several races and when on tour it helped distance them from the Southern Jim Crow Laws if locals believed the band was from another country.

The first white girl to join the band in 1943 was Rosalind "Roz" Cron, a gifted alto saxophonist. The girls toured and stayed on a large bus with kitchen and bathroom as getting lodging in the south was often difficult.

Other notable members were Helen Jones, adopted daughter of Dr. Jones, who played the trombone, Willie Mae Lee Wong and Tiny Davis. In 1941, they cut ties to the school and became professional band. Because they were female in the male dominated jazz field, they rarely got the credit they deserved. The *Chicago Defender* referred to them as "the most prominent and probably best female aggregation of the Big Band era."

Billie Holiday is usually the first name that comes to mind when thinking of jazz singers. She had a successful career, but a troubled life. Born Eleanora Fagan in Philadelphia, Pennsylvania, on April 7, 1915, she grew up in Baltimore. She began singing in nightclubs in Harlem in the early 1930s, and was soon signed to a recording contract with Columbia Records. Her innovative phrasing and style influenced jazz music and pop singing. She was known for her vocal range and improvisational skills. Her first hit single, "Riffin' the Scotch", released in 1935 was a hit. By the 1940s, she was one of the most popular singers in the world. She influenced some of the most famous musicians of the day. Louis Armstrong claimed while she didn't invent the torch song, her voice defined it. Thelonious Monk and Miles Davis also credited Billie Holiday with being the influence for some of their songs. She recorded some of her most famous songs during this period; "Lover Man," and "God Bless the Child."

However, it was a song that was strangely ahead of its time that caused her problems. "Strange Fruit" protesting the lynching of Blacks would have fit the protest music of the 1960s.

She was the subject of three movies, *Lady Sings the Blues*, starring Diana Ross, a lesser-known documentary, *Billie Holiday: Sensational Lady*, and the most recent one, *The United States vs. Billie Holiday.*

Holiday's life was plagued by her addiction to drugs and alcohol. All her biographical movies attest to that, but this latest one tells how her recording of "Strange Fruit" brought the focus and enmity of some of the most powerful men in government against her. Since she could not be arrested for singing "Strange Fruit," the Federal Bureau of Narcotics (FBN) focused on nailing her for drug possession.

Andra Day, who plays Holiday, was nominated by the Academy Award for Best Actress for that role in 2021 and won the Golden Globe Award for Best Actress in a Motion Picture Drama. It was Day's debut performance in a lead role. The film's soundtrack won the Grammy Award for Best Compilation Soundtrack for Visual Media. It's "Tigress and Tweed" was nominated for the Golden Globe Award for Best Original Song.

Throughout her career, Holiday collaborated with many famous jazz musicians, like Lester Young, her friend and band member who nicknamed Holiday "Lady Day." In return, she named Young "Pres" (short for "President of the Tenor Saxophone.") She performed with Benny Goodman for her recording debut in 1933 when they recorded several songs including, "Riffin' the Scotch" and "What a Little Moonlight Can Do." She also recorded with Artie Shaw in 1938. They recorded a number of songs together, including her controversial "Strange Fruit." Holiday's life was troubled; she consistently married or had relationships with abusive men. She struggled with drug addiction and alcoholism and was arrested and sentenced to Alderson Federal Prison Camp in West Virginia for drug possession in 1947. The drug possession conviction caused her to lose her New York City Cabaret Card, so she was not allowed to work anywhere that sold alcohol. Instead, she performed in concerts venues and theaters. There were later drug arrests. The last being just before her death while she was in the hospital.

Despite FBI persecution and her personal problems, Holiday continued to perform and record until her death due to cirrhosis of the liver in 1959. "Strange Fruit" was named "song of the century" by Time Magazine in 1999. She is definitely one of the greatest jazz singers of all time, and her music continues to be played by modern audiences and covered by present day musicians.

She was inducted into the Grammy Hall of Fame, the National Rhythm & Blues Hall of Fame, and the Rock & Roll Hall of Fame.

The Boswell Sisters began as a trio. Martha and Connie—she later used the Connee version—were born in Kansas City, Missouri. Helvetia, nicknamed Vet, was born in Birmingham, Alabama. Their father was a former vaudeville performer. Both he and their mother loved music. The family moved to New Orleans in 1914.

The girls and their brother Clyde Jr. (Clydie) were trained in classical music, but the sisters fell in love with New Orleans jazz. Vet took up the banjo and guitar, and Connie the saxophone and trombone. Martha continued playing the piano but focused on the rhythms and idioms of ragtime and hot jazz.

By 1925, they had formed a group, but were not getting great reviews. One day, while they were preparing for a broadcast engagement, they accidentally hit on the sound that brought them success. That day, Connee had a cold and her voice was weaker. She moved closer to the microphone and sang in her lowered voice. The result was a sound that emphasized the group's unique harmony.

Between 1930 and '35, was when the Boswell Sisters made their most noted recordings. They frequently appearing as guests on radio shows and played in several Hollywood films including, *The Big Broadcast* in 1932 and *Moulin Rouge* in 1934. The sisters were noted for their tight harmonies, instrumental imitations, and several surprising tempo changes within a song. They often changed melodies and style on recordings such as "Shuffle Off to Buffalo." Rather than each singing in an assigned range, alto, soprano, or contralto, they switched, often in the middle of a song and used a technique called Boswellese gibberish where they inserted two-syllable nonsense words—iggle, eggle, uggle, their version of scat singing.

By 1936, Vet and Martha quit the music business while Connee continued as a solo act. As a child, she had polio and used a wheelchair. To compensate, she often appeared onstage in a taller chair and wore a long gown to give the impression that she was standing. Connee also acted in several films during the 1940s and was a regular on the early '50s TV series *Pete Kelly's Blues*, with Jack Webb.

"Shout, Sister, Shout!" became their signature song but my favorite and one of the first jazz songs I remember hearing on the radio as a child was Connee's version of "Basin Street Blues." They also did a version of my dad's iconic "I found a Million Dollar Baby."

Another big name jazz singer, **Ella Fitzgerald**, was born in 1917 in Newport News, Virginia. She began singing in clubs in Harlem in her teens. She was known as the "First Lady of Song," "Queen of Jazz," and "Lady Ella." When asked, she credits Connee Boswell as her biggest influence in music. Some of her early songs have a striking similarity to Boswell's songs. Fitzgerald's first recording was "Love and Kisses," in 1935, followed by her hit single, "A-Tisket, A-Tasket," in 1938 while she was singing with Chick Webb's Orchestra. When Webb, who was also her guardian, died in 1939, she led his band until it broke up in 1942.

Her career was at its peak in the 1940s, when she recorded some of her most famous songs, including "Lady Be Good," "How High the Moon," and "Summertime."

Fitzgerald often improvised scat singing, which worked well in her *Ella and Louis* and *Ella and Louis Again* albums with Louis Armstrong, himself a maestro of scat singing.

She toured with Count Basie and recorded several albums with him, including *Ella and Basie* and *Let's Face the Music and Dance*. They did some sellout concerts together.

Fitzgerald recorded what some consider her most famous albums, the songbook series with Duke Ellington. Her recording of Ellington's "It Don't Mean a Thing (If It Ain't Got That Swing)" shows her a master of swing. Her marriage to Dizzy Gillespie's bass player, Ray Brown, lasted from 1947 to 1953 during which time she recorded several albums with Gillespie, including *Ella and Dizzy and Satchmo and Ella*. With Gillespie, she moved from the big band swing sound to the bebop.

Fitzgerald's versatility earned her credits in the pop field. Her version of "Mack the Knife" was covered by Bobby Darin and others.

Fitzgerald, considered one of the greatest jazz singers of all time, performed until shortly before her death from diabetes in 1996. She also appeared in several movies. She won 13 Grammy Awards, and received the Grammy Lifetime Achievement Award in 1967 and was inducted into the Grammy Hall of Fame, the National Endowment for the Arts Jazz Masters Fellowship, and the Rock and Roll Hall of Fame. President Ronald Reagan awarded her The Presidential Medal of Freedom in 1987.

The 1972 documentary, *Ella Fitzgerald: A Life in Jazz,* tells her story

Lena Horne was born in Brooklyn, New York on June 30, 1917 to affluent mixed race parents. She began her career in the chorus of the Cotton Club when she was sixteen and cut her first record with Noble Sissle's band in 1936. Her grandmother, Cora Calhoun Horne, was an active member of the National Association for the Advancement of Colored People (NAACP) and introduced young Lena to the organization as a child. Throughout her life, she was active in civil and human rights causes. She broke the color barrier in many ways.

The first was in 1940, when she toured with Charlie Barnet's band, one of the first white bandleaders to integrate his band. She was one of the first black performers to achieve mainstream success in Hollywood not cast in a subservient role, when she played in *Stormy Weather* and *Cabin in the Sky* both in 1943. The Lena Horne Show in 1969 was one of the first television variety show hosted by a black woman. The NAACP inducted her into its Hall of Fame with the Image award and for Outstanding Jazz Artist. She earned three Grammy Awards: Lifetime Achievement, Best Jazz Vocalist, and Best Pop Vocalist.

Lena Horne's success as a Black singer and actress who was an outspoken Civil Rights supporter brought her under scrutiny of the highly conservative powers in Washington led by Senator Joseph McCarthy. She was blacklisted in Hollywood during the McCarthy era, even though she was never a member of the Communist Party.

During that time, she got few film roles and performed mostly in nightclubs or theaters. The harassment never stopped her from speaking out against racism and injustice. Eventually, McCarthyism lost its power, and she resumed her film career in the late 1950s. Her role opposite Richard Widmark in the 1969 film *Death of a Gunfighter,* where she played a frontier madam, again caused a controversy as some Black people didn't like her playing the part of a shady character. Her best-known song and one that reflected her own life was "Stormy Weather." She is also remembered for her versions of "Honeysuckle Rose" and "Black Coffee."

Sarah Vaughan was born in Newark, New Jersey on March 27, 1924. She took piano lessons beginning at age seven. Her family was active in their church, so she began singing and playing piano in the church choir as a child. By her mid-teens, she was illegally performing in some Newark nightclubs. Her first real break came in 1942 when she won an amateur night contest at the Apollo Theater in Harlem, New York. Part of the prize was performing at the theater. Later that year, she returned to perform at the Apollo opening for Ella Fitzgerald.

Her professional career began with singing with Earl Hines's band which included some of the pioneers in bebop; singer, Billy Eckstine; trumpeter Dizzy Gillespie; and saxophonist Charlie Parker. She stayed with Hines for two years, where she developed her own unique style of singing, a combination of jazz, blues, and gospel.

Billy Eckstine left to form his own band in 1943, taking Gillespie and Parker. Vaughan left Hines's band in 1944, to join Billy Eckstine's orchestra which played much more in the bebop style. Vaughan quickly adapted to this new and exciting style of jazz. She became one of Eckstine's most popular singers.

In 1945, she began a solo career. She recorded over 70 albums, toured all over the world, and collaborated with some of the biggest names in jazz, including Miles Davis, Duke Ellington, and Dizzy Gillespie. Being an accomplished pianist, she often wrote her own arrangements for her performances. She often used scat singing in her songs. When asked how she classified her talent, she replied, "I never thought of myself as a jazz singer. I just sang the songs that I loved." Her voice range lent itself to pop ballads as jazz became less popular. Several of her songs were successful on the pop charts including, "That Lucky Old Sun," "Rainy Days and Mondays," and "Send in the Clowns."

Vaughan was a role model for African American women, and her success helped to break down racial barriers in the music industry. From her bluesy "Mean to Me" to the uptempo "Misty," she shows an incredible vocal range and ability to improvise.

In 1989, on her final recording, the Quincy Jones album *Back on the Block,* she performs a brief scatting duet with Ella Fitzgerald. This was her only studio recording with Fitzgerald in a career that had begun 46 years earlier opening for Fitzgerald at the Apollo. She died in 1990 at the age of 66. She is considered one of the greatest jazz singers of all time.

The Andrews Sisters, Laverne, Maxene, and Patty Andrews, who were known for their close harmonies and upbeat swing tunes. Their career peaked during World War II, when they were known as "The Sweethearts of the USA." for songs about American troops like "Boogie Woogie Bugle Boy," "Don't Sit Under the Apple Tree (With Anyone Else but Me)," and "A Hot Time In the Town of Berlin." They performed in service comedy films, such as *Buck Privates* and *Private Buckaroo*. The sisters were born in Minneapolis, Minnesota, to Greek and Norwegian parents began a singing together as children, encouraged by their mother. In the early 1930s, they began performing in vaudeville shows and on radio and signed with Decca Records in 1937. Their first hit single, "Bei Mir Bist Du Schön," was a Yiddish song that translates to "To Me, You Are Beautiful."

The Andrews Sisters entertaining troops all over the world. After the war, they continued to record and perform and had several more hit singles, including, "I'll Be Seeing You" and "The White Cliffs of Dover." From 1944 to 1951. They hosted their own radio show. The Andrews Sisters disbanded in 1953 in feuds over money. They attempted solo careers, which never took off. They were inducted into the Vocal Group Hall of Fame in 1998 and the Rock and Roll Hall of Fame in 2010. Their music veered out of classic jazz into other genre. Their 1941 hit "Boogie Woogie Bugle Boy" is an early example of rhythm and blues.

Eunice Kathleen Waymon may not ring any bells. But performing under the name **Nina Simone** her music spanned styles from gospel and classical, to folk, blues, jazz, R&B, and pop. She began playing piano at the age of three or four. The first song she learned was "God Be With You, Till We Meet Again.". The gospel song was appropriate since she played at her local church. Her classical concert debut occurred when she was 12. It was here that her Civil Rights and protest songs may have taken root because, at this concert her parents, who were seated in the front row, were made to move to the back of the hall and their seats given to white people. Simone refused to play until her parents were moved back to their original seats.

After her high school graduation in 1950, she spent time at the Julliard School. She applied for an audition at the Curtis Institute of Music in Philadelphia. They denied her application there. She felt it was for racial reasons; the school said it was not.

It was then when she began playing in a local nightclub that she changed her name since her parents did not approve of jazz or R&B music. She was still trying to get into classical but began building a following with her other music. Her recording of George Gershwin's "I Loves You, Porgy" (from Porgy and Bess), became her only Billboard top 20 hit in the United States.

It was the song she wrote and performed as an answer to the murder of Medgar Evers and the September 15, 1963 bombing of the 16th Street Baptist Church in Birmingham, Alabama, that killed four young black girls and partly blinded a fifth. "Mississippi Goddam" was her response that she felt was "like throwing ten bullets back at them." They boycotted the song in some southern states. From that point on, she became an ardent Civil Right activist. Her views were more in line with Malcolm X than Dr. King. Her career deteriorated, since many record companies would not record her. She moved overseas and was diagnosed with bipolar disorder. She died in France on April 21, 2003.

She and Thelonious Monk are honored with "Thelonious Monk's San Juan Hill, Nina Simone's Lincoln Square," exhibit at Lincoln Center for the Performing Arts in New York City.

When you visit Birmingham, the Alabama Jazz Hall of Fame and historic Carver Theatre are must-sees. The museum is undergoing renovatins and will reopen in 2024, but the theatre is still promoting love of jazz. It opened in 1935 as a movie house and was a hub for nightlife in Birmingham's Black Business District during the Jim Crow era.

International Sweethearts album cover at Tennessee State Museum, Nashville

Chapter 10 Country

On my 14th birthday, my parents woke me with my present, a small, square, boxy record player playing a 78 record of a country song I had not heard before, "Jack of Diamonds." At this time, I didn't listen to country music much. I was already a blues fan, liked jazz to dance to, and rapidly becoming an avid rock and roller.

Like mostly every other teenage girl in the country, I was in love with Elvis Presley. His recently released "Heartbreak Hotel" had my hormones raging. I loved the record player and soon acquired Elvis's next release, "Hound Dog," and "Don't be Cruel." About two years later, when I heard George Jones singing, "Window Up Above," I truly appreciated country music.

It was evident even to my younger self that country music was highly influenced by the blues and a contributor to rock and roll. It officially began in 1927 and continues to this day. There are so many musicians that helped create and perpetuate this genre, I could never get them all in one book, let alone a single chapter.

US Congress officially recognized Bristol, Tennessee-Virginia as the "Birthplace of Country Music" in 1998. They earned this title because of a two-week recording session for Victor Talking Machine Company in 1927. Ralph Peer, a Victor representative, placed ads looking for "Hillbilly Singers" as country music was called then, for what became known as the "Bristol Sessions." The place to start your journey is the Birthplace of Country Music Museum. The Museum tells the story of the famous 1927 Bristol Sessions. It's done with videos and interactive exhibits where you can listen, mix, and even record your own versions of the songs from that session.

Ralph Peer, who was a producer for Victor Talking Machine Company, later RCA Victor, wanted to record "Hillbilly music" using the newest electrical recording equipment developed in 1925. He asked Ernest Stoneman, who was already playing and recording that music with his wife, Hattie, where would be the best place to set up recording sessions? He decided on Bristol because with Johnson City and Kingsport, Tennessee, it formed the Tri-Cities, then the largest urban area in the Appalachians, an area surrounded by musicians who played this type of music. At the sessions, Peer recorded 76 songs by 19 performers or groups.

Remember, although due to segregation and Jim Crow laws, music was classified by race, there was already a big crossover of music. The banjo, an African instrument, was common in "Hillbilly bands" of the time. The blues, considered "race music," melded into much so-called white music. El Watson was the lone African American artist to record at Bristol Sessions. He recorded "Pot Licker Blues" and "Narrow Gauge Blues" backed by white musician Charles Johnson, who played guitar on Watson's recordings. Watson returned the favor, played bones on a few songs recorded by the Johnson Brothers. These are some of the earliest integrated recordings of country music. When Peer returned to Bristol in 1928 to record more musicians, another African American act was a duo Tarter & Gay. Like Watson, they recorded two sides, "Brownie Blues" and "Unknown Blues." They were all labeled race records, not country.

The music of the Appalachians moved out into the country as a whole and merged with the sounds of the blues and even some Native American songs, if you consider Hank Williams' "Kaw-liga" and "Running Bear," sung by Johnny Preston and later Sonny James. It was written by rocker, The Big Bopper. One of the saddest but true songs is Johnny Cash's "Ballad of Ira Hayes." "Seminole Wind" by John Anderson retells the story of the one tribe who never surrendered.

Much of the music that evolved in the mountains of Appalachia has crossed genres and blended with many cultures, that it is difficult to classify a singer or a song as "country." However, two of the recorded musicians at the Bristol Sessions are credited with the birth of country music, Jimmie Rogers and The Carter Family.

Jimmie Rodgers is known as "The Father of Country Music." He's also called "The Singing Brakeman," and "The Blue Yodeler." He was born James Charles Rodgers September 8, 1897, in Pine Springs, Mississippi, just north of Meridian. Much of his music resembled the blues and there's some crossover with jazz. Louis Armstrong played trumpet in Jimmie Rodgers' "Blue Yodel #9." Like his music, his life is a mix of triumphs and tragedies. His mother died when he was around six. By 13 he organized singing troupes and ran away twice. His father brought him back, and eventually he went to work for the railroad. It was here he heard the songs of the Gandy Dancers, African-American railroad workers who installed the rails, that were later part of his music. In 1924, he was diagnosed with tuberculous. It ended his railroad job and left him free to pursue his music. By then, he was married and had fathered two daughters. One died at only six months old. He moved his wife and remaining daughter to Asheville, North Carolina. Things were tough financially. He worked as a janitor, cab driver, and detective until April 1927, when he and Otis Kuykendall performed for the first time on WWNC, Asheville's first radio station. Jimmy later recruited a group from Bristol, Tennessee, named the Tenneva Ramblers. They got a weekly show on WWNC.

Members of the Tenneva Ramblers told Rogers about Peer's ad. He applied and recorded two songs that were only moderately successful, "The Soldier's Sweetheart" and "Sleep, Baby, Sleep." Peer saw Rogers' potential and offered him another session and that November he traveled to Camden, New Jersey and recorded four more songs. One of them, "Blue Yodel," better known as "T for Texas," featured his trademark yodel and sold nearly half a million copies over the next two years. His name was made in the music business. He built his reputation further when he did a movie short for Columbia Pictures, *The Singing Brakeman,* and on July 16, 1930, he recorded "Blue Yodel No. 9" with Louis Armstrong on trumpet and Armstrong's wife Lil on piano.

His health was declining as his fame was rising. His last recordings were made in May 1933 where he recorded "Years Ago." He was so weak, he needed a nurse to accompany him. He died while there for the session at the Taft Hotel in New York City on May 26, 1933 from a pulmonary hemorrhage caused by his tuberculosis. He was 35 years old. His body was sent back to Meridian, Mississippi where he was buried in Oak Grove Cemetery. His music lives on and has been covered by many singers.

In 2013, Jimmie Rogers was posthumously inducted into the Blues Hall of Fame. This blending of genres ran both ways. Howlin' Wolf tried to copy Rodgers' yodeling and created his own howling sound.

A. P. Carter was a traveling salesman along with other jobs. It seems like that is the furthest thing from a country music career, yet **The Carter Family** became the first vocal group to become country music stars and were integral in the development of country music. They are known as "The First Family of Country Music." Here's why. A. P. had a hobby. While he traveled around, he collected old folk songs. Remember, this was when radio and phonograph records were just beginning, especially in the Appalachian area where hardly anyplace had electricity. The Carter family, like other families there, would play these old folk songs on their cabin porches at night to the accompaniment of a fiddle, dulcimer, guitar, or banjo.

When A. P. heard about Ralph Peer's ad for hillbilly singers, he convinced his wife, Sara, and his sister-in-law, Maybelle, to go to Bristol and try for a recording contract. They recorded six songs including "Wandering Boy," "Poor Orphan Child," "The Storms Are on the Ocean," and "Single Girl, Married Girl." They were paid $50 for each song and a half cent royalty on each copy sold. By the end of 1930, they had sold 300,000 records.

A. P. continued collecting folk songs, traveling with **Lesley Riddle**, better known as Esley. He had an uncanny ability to memorize the melody of a song while A. P. wrote the lyrics. They would take the songs back to the Carter home and A. P. would fiddle a little with the lyrics and Riddle would teach the melody to Sara and Maybelle.

Riddle was an African American musician who had been injured in a work accident and had his right leg amputated at the knee. Shortly after that, he was involved in a fight with his uncle involving a shotgun the two men argued over. The gun discharged while Lesley's right hand was over the barrel, causing him to lose his middle and ring fingers of the hand. Neither injury slowed Riddle's playing. Because of these missing fingers he adjusted his picking techniques to use only his thumb, index and little finger giving him an unusual picking and slide style. He used his index finger to play the melody and his thumb to keep the rhythm on the bass strings. Maybelle credits his technique with developing her unique Carter Scratch style of guitar playing.

When the Carter family recorded, Sara sang lead and played rhythm guitar or autoharp, Maybelle sang harmony and played lead guitar, A. P. sometimes sang background or harmony and occasionally lead. Often his voice fades as he had a habit of wandering around the studio sometimes too far from the microphones to have his voice picked up.

Overall, the Carter family made 144 records for Victor and its subsidiaries over the next seven years. They made around the same number of recordings for other labels between 1935 and 1940. Sara and A. P. divorced but continued to record together until 1944.

Many of the Carter Family songs have become famous classics like "Wabash Cannonball," "Can the Circle Be Unbroken," "Wildwood Flower," "Keep On the Sunny Side," and "I'm Thinking Tonight of My Blue Eyes." Interestingly, while they were playing at a station in Mexico with a very distant range, Sara sang "I'm Thinking Tonight of My Blue Eyes" supposedly to let a former lover know she was divorced from A. P. and was missing him. It worked as he rejoined her, and they were married just a few weeks later.

After the original group disbanded, Maybelle continued performing and recording with her daughters, Anita, Helen, and June. They performed under various names, "The Carter Sisters and Mother Maybelle." "The Carter Sisters," or "Mother Maybelle and the Carter Sisters." Chet Atkins began playing electric guitar for them in 1949. When the Grand Ole Opry invited Mother Maybelle and the Carter Sisters to become members, they didn't want Chet Atkins. When the Carters insisted it was all or none, they accepted him.

Sara died in 1979, A. P. in 1960, and Maybelle in 1978. The circle is still unbroken. Descendants of the Carter Family still perform today including John Carter Cash, son of June Carter Cash and Johnny Cash and grandson of Maybelle Carter, and Dale Jett, A.P. and Sara Carter's grandson along with John's then-wife Laura Cash.

There are some terrific places I visited along what is known as The Crooked Road, a 253-mile trail through some of southwest Virginia's music history. It has signs for Wayside Exhibits. There are a series of 26 Wayside Exhibits along the Trail. You can pull off the road to read the panels and listen on your vehicle radio to a five-minute audio recording about the heritage music and musicians in that location. The audio can be heard on your car radio within a range of about one-half mile. They tell a bit of the music history of that spot and play some of the signature songs.

One of the most interesting places along the Crooked Road is the Carter Family Fold, a non-profit founded by Janette Carter, A. P. and Sara Carter's daughter with a Saturday night tradition that keeps the music begun by her family alive. The Fold is in Hiltons, at the base of Clinch Mountain. It's a rustic frame building constructed in 1976 and expanded over the years. It has garage type doors along the sides that can open in hot weather to cool the building. Normally only acoustic bands perform, and electric instruments are rarely permitted. The band playing the first time I visited was Twin Creeks Stringband, an old-time mountain music group composed of Jared Boyd on claw-hammer banjo and vocal, Chris Prillaman on fiddle, Jason Hambrick playing guitar and vocal, and Stacy Boyd backing it up on his bass. They had us and many other guests dancing to tunes like "The Long Black Veil" and "Cotton Eye Joe."

Two other treasures are located at the Carter Family Fold. The cabin that was the birthplace of A.P. Carter was moved there from its original location in Little Valley, the next valley parallel to Poor Valley, where the Fold is. When I entered, the first one that greeted me was a cute dog named Wilson, the Fold's mascot. Later, I saw him "dancing" to the music with other guests on the dance floor. US Registry service dogs are allowed at the concerts.

The two-room log cabin with a tin roof and stone chimney was built in the mid-1800s. It is furnished much as it would have been when A.P. was a child. There are old family photos, clothing, spices, mason jars, and early 20th century furniture. The white enamel gas stove had old cooking pots and an aluminum coffee pot on it.

The other treasure is A.P.'s store. Along with his music career, he ran this store almost to the time of his death in 1960. It was where the first Fold concerts were held prior to building the concert hall. It's a State and National Historic Landmark. When I stepped into the white frame building with its twin peaked tin roofs, there are lots of memorabilia from the Carters' career. There's an old gramophone, dresses Sara and Maybelle wore at a 59th year anniversary performance, the Carter family tree, and more. It's treasure trove of musical memories.

The first weekend of August the Fold hosts a Saturday festival. There are craftsmen, lots of good country cooking, and naturally music. When I attended the festival, I heard a couple of amazing bands, Carson Peters & Iron Mountain, and Whitetop Mountain Band. The youngest member of Whitetop Mountain Band, a lady named Martha Spencer, had her pet Yorkie named Minnie Pearl with her and carried her on the dance floor when she danced.

George Hay opened the WSM Barn Dance, which became The Grand Ole Opry on November 28, 1925, with old-time fiddler, Uncle Jimmy Thompson. It became the Holy Grail of country music. Ryman Auditorium, which housed the Opry from 1943 to 1974, is still called the "Mother Church of Country Music." Acceptance on the Opry, meant you had arrived in the world of country music.

The Grand Ole Opry got on my radar around 1958. After hearing George Jones, I was hungry for more. Since my parents had a set bedtime for us kids, I would plug my radio in and hide it under my pillow on Saturday nights.

A note about radios of that time, every self-respecting teen carried one of those "new" portable radios. They were about 10 inches wide, seven inches high, and about four inches thick. They had plastic cases, usually in pastel colors, and played either on four C batteries or one of those square batteries. You could also use them with a standard plug at home. We took them whenever we went to the beach or anywhere where we would be sitting around and wanted to listen to Elvis or any music. They fit nicely under my pillow and I set the volume so I could hear it when I laid my head on the pillow, but my mom or dad couldn't when they came in to say good night.

I listened not only to the Opry but Ernest Tubb's Record Shop which followed and often to Ralph Emory, who was a Nashville disk jockey with an all night show that played all the latest country Music records and lots of gossip about the stars. Often a musician would drop in and talk with him on the air. Radio show disk jockeys were much more informal then. I got to know Minnie Pearl and her famous "Howdeee," Grampa Jones, Stringbean, and all the singers on the Opry.

Before the Opry caught my attention, The Fruit Jar Drinkers with **Uncle Dave Macon** became the Opry's first real star. Uncle Dave was best known for his lively style. He would often stomp, kick, and shout. He recorded over 170 songs between 1924 and 1938. One, "Rock About My Saro Jane" was a style he learned from black stevedores working along the Cumberland River in the 1880s. His "Buddy Won't You Roll Down the Line" was inspired by the Coal Creek War in the 1890s. Along with Roy Acuff, he played a part in the Republic Pictures movie *Grand Ole Opry*. There's lots of reasons why Knoxville, Tennessee is known as the Cradle of country Music. Sterchi Brothers Furniture there acted as agents for Aeolian - Vocalian Record Co. and helped Uncle Dave Macon get his start. The store location is number 10 on the Cradle of Country Music Tour.

When you visit the Opry today, you'll notice more focus on the singer than the band. You can thank **Roy Acuff** for that. He is known as the "King of Country Music." Roy Acuff's earliest musical performances were as an entertainer for a quack selling patent medicines to cure all illnesses. Roy would sing and draw a crowd and the "Doctor" would go into his spiel about what the medicine would do.

He next formed a group with guitarist Jess Easterday and Hawaiian guitarist, Clell Summey, which he originally called the Tennessee Crackerjacks. They performed on WNOX's live country music variety show "The Midday Merry-Go-Round." The show was broadcast from the top floor of the Andrew Johnson Hotel in Knoxville. His fiddle is in the Museum of East Tennessee History. Another exhibit there is "They Sang What They Lived: The Story of **Carl and Pearl Butle**r" singers of the Number one hit, "Don't Let Me Cross Over."

The Andrew Johnson Hotel is known for another event in country music history. It was where Hank Williams spent the part of the last night of his life. He reportedly had a shot of morphine and some liquor with his dinner and was escorted out late that night in a wheelchair in order to make the next concert in Canton, Ohio on time. The hotel became decrepit over the years and was converted to office spaces. It had a reincarnation and is re-opening in 2024 as a new luxury hotel. Its musical heritage will be honored with three music venues, including a rooftop bar tentatively called Ivories, that will feature jazz.

According to Haunted Knoxville Ghost Tours, Hank's spirit still visits the Andrew Johnson Hotel. Visitors to the building reported seeing a man wearing a cowboy hat and one visitor reported sharing an elevator and that man who looked like Hank. The visitor turned to look at the man when the elevator stopped and the doors opened and the man was gone. The hotel merits a marker on the Cradle of Country Music Tour.

Acuff's band grew and changed over the next few years. Acuff's recording of "The Great Speckled Bird" landed them a contract with American Record Corporation, including Acuff's best-known song, "Wabash Cannonball. "

In 1936, Roy Acuff and his band wanted out of the American Record contract. They had signed for a 20-song commitment, so they included a somewhat ribald song called "When Lulu's Gone" under a pseudonym, the Bang Boys, to help fulfill the needed number. Interesting both "Wabash Cannonball," and "When Lulu's Gone" are slightly altered version of old Appalachian Folk songs. "When Lulu's Gone" was sung as "Bang Bang Rosie" in Ireland, and evolved to "Bang Away Lulu" in Appalachia. The original song would have an obvious explicit word that is not sung, instead the singer goes directly to the chorus. For example;

> Lulu had two boyfriends,
> Both were very rich,
> One was the son of a banker,
> And the other was a son of a...
>
> Bang Bang my Lulu,
> bang her good and strong...

As early as 1882, a version of "Wabash Cannonball" was played by the mountain folks. The earlier version called "The Great Rock Island Route" was credited to J. A. Roff. William Kindt changed it in 1904 to "Wabash Cannon Ball" All versions including Acuff's contain a variation of this chorus:

Now listen to the jingle, and the rumble, and the roar,

> As she dashes thro' the woodland, and speeds along the shore,
> See the mighty rushing engine, hear her merry bell ring out,
> As they speed along in safety, on the "Great Rock-Island Route."

Roy Acuff and the Smokey Mountain Boys' version is listed as one of 500 songs that shaped rock and roll at the Rock and Roll Hall of Fame in Cleveland, Ohio. It's been recorded by singers as varied as Bing Crosby and blues singer, Blind Willie McTell. Acuff recorded a version of the Cajun song, "Jole Blon" on the Nitty Gritty Dirt Band album, "Will the Circle Be Unbroken." It's all an example of the merging of different genres in music.

Acuff partnered with Fred Rose to form Acuff-Ross Music in 1942 which signed some of the biggest names in country music including, Hank Williams. Acuff's life-sized statue sits on a bench with Minnie Pearl at Ryman Auditorium.

One early Opry musician who has gotten little of the recognition he deserves is **DeFord Bailey**. He was the first performer to be introduced on Nashville radio station WSM's Barn Dance the night it was first called the Grand Ole Opry, the first African-American performer to appear on the show, and the first performer to have his music recorded in Nashville on October 2, 1928, when he recorded "Ice Water Blues" and "Davidson County Blues" for Victor records. Yes, he was also a blues musician.

His instrument of choice was the harmonica which he used to recreate many sounds especially the sound of a train horn which is prominent in his "Pan American Blues," the first recording of a harmonica blues solo. He appeared regularly on Grand Ole Opry until he was fired over a dispute about playing ASCAP (American Society of Composers, Authors, and Publishers) music that was then banned in favor of the new company, BMI (Broadcast Music, Inc.) DeFord Bailey was invited back to the Opry in 1974, when he appeared for a special event to mark the Opry leaving the Ryman Auditorium for the Grand Ole Opry House. He appeared several times after this.

One of the most long-lived musicians on the Grand Ole Opry was James Cecil Dickens better known as **Little Jimmy Dickens**. Although he stood only 4'11" in his glamorous rhinestone-studded outfits, he was a giant in the music industry. He was born in Bolt, West Virginia on December 19, 1920, and by the late 1930s began his music career. It carried him to the height of country music fame when Roy Acuff helped him get a Columbia Recording contract and a place on the Grand Ole Opry in 1948. He is best remembered for his comedy songs such as "Take an Old Cold Tater (And Wait)" which earned him the nickname "Tater" from Hank Williams. His biggest hit was "May the Bird of Paradise Fly Up Your Nose." It charted at number 1 on the country chart and number 15 on the pop chart. In 1964, he became the first country music entertainer to go on a world tour. His highest honor was being elected to the County Music Hall of Fame. At the age of 90, Little Jimmy became the oldest living member and sometimes host of the Grand Ole Opry.

Another new style came into country music in the 1950s. **Ernest Tubb** was the innovator of honky tonk sound. He blended sounds of western swing with a full rhythm section playing a two-beat rhythm, a strong backbeat, and steel guitar and fiddle as the dominant instruments. He wasn't the first. Jelly Roll Morton and other jazz musicians had used a honky tonk sound with boogie-woogie piano style. Later musicians like Fats Domino would use it in rock and roll songs of the late 1950s.

Born in 1914 in a small town near Dallas, Texas, Tubb was a rabid Jimmie Rodgers fan. He learned to play guitar and yodel in Jimmie Rodgers style and at age 19, he got a job as a singer on KONO-AM in San Antonio. He contacted Mrs. Jimmie Rodgers, who also lived in San Antonio, and asked for an autographed photo of his idol. She liked the young singer even though he didn't sound anything like her deceased husband. She let him use Rodger's guitar and helped him get a contract with RCA Records in 1936, but advised him to develop his own style.

Ernest made several singles with RCA, including "The Passing of Jimmie Rodgers" and "The Last Thoughts of Jimmie Rodgers" still trying to imitate Rodgers. They didn't do well, and soon he was back on the road in Texas searching for whatever gigs he could get. Tonsillitis cost him his tonsils, but probably saved his career. In 1939, severe infection forced the operation and thereafter he could not yodel.

He adapted a drawling, narrative type of singing that secured got him a contract with the new Decca label and began to record again in 1940. The first of Ernest Tubb's Decca singles sold fairly well, but in 1941, when he released a song he had written himself, "I'm Walking the Floor Over You," he was suddenly a superstar. It sold 400,000 copies the first year and millions since then.

One thing Ernest Tubb is known for was the helping hand he offered newcomers to the music field. He helped not only his own son, Justin Tubb, but he aided others to stardom including Johnny Cash, Patsy Cline, Skeeter Davis, Jack Greene, George Hamilton IV, Stonewall Jackson, Loretta Lynn, Carl Smith, Hank Snow, the Wilburn Brothers, and Hank Williams.

Tubb played in several movies and TV shows and was a long-time member of the Grand Ole Opry. He died in 1984 but his songs and memory live on.

Perhaps the first name that comes to mind when someone says "Country Music," is **Hank Williams.** Named Hiram, Williams was born in the midst of the depression in Butler County, Alabama. His father was hospitalized due to an injury for most of Williams' young life and his mother supported the family, running a series of boarding houses and working as a night-shift nurse in the local hospital. By the time Hank was a teen, they lived in Georgiana, about 60 miles from Montgomery.

It was here that Williams learned to play guitar. He met Rufus "Tee-Tot" Payne, an African American street performer. Payne gave young Hank guitar lessons which he paid for with money he earned shining shoes or selling newspapers or meals his mother, Lillie, cooked. Payne played mostly blues and he taught Hank chords, chord progressions, bass turns, and a musical style Hank would use in most of his future songwriting that blended blues with Country. When Hank recorded "My Bucket's Got a Hole in It" in 1949, he credited Payne taught it to him. When Hank moved to Montgomery in 1937, he lost contact with Payne.

Hank won a talent contest at the Montgomery Empire Theater singing an original song entitled "WPA Blues" in December 1937. There was no stopping his music career from that moment. He worked local clubs and did a show on WSFA, a Montgomery radio station. He began doing shows from Western Georgia to the Florida Panhandle. His mother managed the band, and they played theaters before movies and honky tonk bars. Unfortunately, here Hank's love of alcohol developed. He was born with spina bifida occulta, which was painful, leading to his addiction to first alcohol and later prescription medicine.

Some of his most remembered songs are "I'm So Lonesome I Could Cry," "Your Cheatin' Heart," and "Jambalaya (On the Bayou)." Ironically, his last release was "I'll Never Get Out of this World Alive" recorded in June 1952 just months before his death, from a combination of alcohol and prescription drugs, en route to a performance on Jan 1, 1953. The last place anyone saw him alive was Burger Bar in Bristol where his driver stopped in front and asked Hank if he wanted something to eat. He replied, "no."

Another child was born in 1918 in the tiny hamlet of Elmore, just about 15 miles north of Montgomery, Alabama. His life was destined to link with Hank's in the creation of the most enduring legend country music has ever known. On the 50th anniversary year of Hank Williams' death, I had the honor of meeting this man who knew Williams well. William Herbert **"Lum" York** was a musician best known as the bass player in Hank Williams' Drifting Cowboys from 1944 to 1949. Lum was very generous with sending me photos and giving honest recollections of his time playing with Hank.

I met him at the Hank Williams Museum in Montgomery, which is a wonderful place to learn more about Hank Williams. My favorite exhibit there is his blue Cadillac. Montgomery is filled with memories of Hank. A life-size statue of him stands in the center of the Riverfront Entertainment District, plus his burial site is in the Oakwood Cemetery Annex.

From 1944, their stories mesh, so I'll tell their joint stories as Lum told them to me.

In rural Alabama, the depression days of the 1930s and early '40s were rough. Lum remembered, "I only had two pairs of overalls. My mother washed on Wednesdays, so I had to wear them all week long."

Lum was a schoolboy before they moved to a house with electricity. But life was more than just the backbreaking work of picking cotton and tilling the vegetable patch. On Saturday nights when the family gathered around the radio playing the Grand Ole Opry, York's lifelong love of music was born. When he was 12, his older brother bought a guitar. When his brother joined the army, Lum bought his guitar for fifty cents. Within a year, York had taught himself to play by listening to the radio.

Much like Hank, who dropped out of school when he was 16 so that he could work full time, York had to drop out of school to help his mother after his father died. He worked with the CCC, Roosevelt's Civilian Conservation Program, designed to help stimulate the economy by allowing boys and young men to work on public buildings and parks for a small salary plus room and board.

When Lum returned from the CCC camp, he would hitchhike into town to hear the local bands play. Since he had no money to buy a ticket, he filched eggs from his mother's chicken house and sold them to local groceries for the admission price. He had heard Hank on the radio and began to hang around the station. They first met in 1939. The friendship remained throughout Hank' life.

In 1944 Lum and his big bass fiddle joined Hank's band, The Drifting Cowboys. York told of the first time he played music with Hank, "We had got to be friends working together in the shipyard. One night, I went to where he was playing. I had bought a bass and was learning to play it. I was also friends with the guy who was playing bass that night and he asked me to sit in while he went to the bathroom. Hank and Audrey were dancing while I played the set. When the music ended, Hank asked me 'You want a job playing with the band?' I told him, 'Hank, I don't know how to play too good.' He said, 'You want to learn? I'll pay you $20 a week and room and board.'" Until 1948, Lum drove around the South with Hank and the band. Sometimes there was only one other member, the trumpet player.

As Hank's popularity and his income increased, he acquired a tiny trailer to pull around to shows. Audrey often joined them then, and they were treated to "home cooked" meals. It also gave them a place to lie down and rest between the shows.

During this time, Lillie, Hank's mother, often traveled with them and managed a "junior band" which would play in the same area as Hank's band. One member of this band, on hearing York's strong southern accent, nicknamed him "Lum." He took the name from a popular radio show comedy duet called *Lum and Abner*. The name stuck.

Since Hank couldn't smoke when he was singing, he liked Lum to stand next to him to play. Lum would light up a cigarette, take a draw, and start playing, then Hank would take the cigarette as he had breaks in the song and finish it. Lum commented, "I was lighting a half a pack of cigs a night and hardly getting a smoke. I told Hank to leave my cigs alone, but as usual, he did the same thing and I kicked his hand. He went ahead and smoked it and grinned. However, I don't recall him smoking another one of my cigs."

Being young, attractive, and somewhat wild, Hank was a big attraction to the ladies. At one show in a small honky tonk on the edge of Montgomery, Hank and Lum were playing to just two couples. Hank spoke to the woman who worked the bar, and she spoke to one of the women at the table. Soon, the two men at the table went to the restroom. Lum recalls Hank telling him "let's go" and they hurried out to the car. The two women were lying down on the back car seats. At the first red light, Lum jumped out and told Hank, "You can get shot if you want to, but I'm going home." He never heard anymore about the incident.

The two men also collaborated on writing songs. Lum wrote the chorus and title of "Take this Message to My Mother" and Hank wrote the verses. Lum was also the unwitting inspiration for Hank's "I Saw the Light." Hank, Audrey, and the band, six people altogether, were crammed into a 1942 Chevy. As you can imagine, it was hard for any of them to rest comfortably. Lum was resting against another player's shoulder, and raised up to change positions. He looked out the window and as he lay back down, he stated, "We're getting close to Montgomery. I saw the light." Referring to a beacon light near town that was always a landmark for the band as they returned home from shows. Hank mumbled that it was a good title for a song and by the next day when the band gathered for their show on WSFA, he was picking out the tune to "I saw the Light." Many versions about the origin of this song have been advanced over the years, but Lum told me this is the true one.

It was around this time that Hank suggested to Lum he might be good as a comedian. Lum stated, "That's one big difference between country music now and then. Those days, every band carried a comedian. Today, they don't do that. But young people still like to hear jokes and stuff."

After the first night, Hank told Lum he didn't think the comedy would work but, Lum decided to make it work. He put on an outrageous country bumpkin outfit, wore a wig, painted freckles on his face and used every joke he could beg, borrow, or steal. It was an unqualified hit, especially with the children in the audience.

When Hank went to the Louisiana Hayride in 1948, Lum was the only player from Montgomery to go with him. He told me, "One thing about Hank, he never closed his shows without singing a hymn. There was always complete reverence with him and the band members at this time. Another thing, he never turned his back on the audience. He always stood facing or to the side."

When Hank was invited into the Grand Ole Opry in 1949, they required him to use the house band on stage. Lum remained behind and played with the staff band on the Hayride. Lum played bass in Lefty Frizzell's band until 1953. He also played for Bill Monroe, who I'll tell you more about in the bluegrass section.

He was on the road when he learned of Hank's death. When I asked about that time, Lum replied, "I was playing with Lefty (Frizzell) then, and we were playing San Antonio, Texas. We were off for a few days and I had gone to Baton Rouge, Louisiana, but had to return to San Antonio the next day. Mrs. Williams called my mother trying to find me, but they didn't know where I was. She wanted me to be a pallbearer, but I had to go back to work. I couldn't let Lefty down and we had to play in Texas."

Lum played with so many other Nashville greats for several years. He returned to Baton Rouge, Louisiana and married Juanita (Nita) Kelly in 1954. (He was married before, for a brief time in the early 50s, to Aline Coates Gibson, also of Baton Rouge.) As a married man, he needed a bit more stability than the music world offered, so he went to work for the Louisiana School Board. Of course, he always played his music on the weekends.

No matter who Lum was playing with, be it George Morgan, Goldie Hill, Marty Robbins, Tennessee Ernie Ford, Hank Thompson, Kitty Wells, Johnny and Jack, Webb Pierce, Slim Whitman, Jimmie Davis, and countless other country music greats, he always remained what he was originally, a plain Southern farm boy.

When asked about his biggest regret in life, Lum told me, "on October 2, 1952 Hank Williams made his last appearance in Baton Rouge, Louisiana I played on the show with him and then later that night he asked me to rejoin his band and play comedian. I told him I would call him back. It was a number at a hotel. I called him back and told him I was going to stay with Lefty. I always regretted that."

Lum performed as a guest performer whenever a country musician played nearby almost until his death and was a fan favorite at the Hank Williams festival in Georgiana, Alabama. As he could no longer play the bass due to a heart condition, he played the spoons.

Before his death, Lum created two tapes: *My Life and Times with Hank Williams* and *Memories are Forever.* He retired from the school board and lived quietly with his wife until his death in 2004. He died in Baton Rouge at age 85 and is buried in Green Oaks Memorial Park.

There are a lot of similarities between Hank Williams and **Lefty Frizzell** besides their honky tonk style. He was born William Orville Frizzell on March 31, 1928 in Corsicana, Texas. His father worked as a roughneck in the oilfield and the family moved around the east Texas oilfields following the jobs. At twelve, he was playing guitar and writing songs. Four years later he started his own band and began playing local bars. By 17, he was married, but still running wild. Lefty was charged with statutory rape of an underage teenage girl and ended up in the local prison.

Lefty cut his first record, "If You've Got the Money (I've Got the Time)," in the summer of 1950. It became a big hit, and by 1951, he had seven of the top 30 hits. In 1951 and 1952, he toured with Hank Williams, doing a bunch of one-nighters. Both young singers loved their booze, so as you can imagine, those tours were wild. Lefty said the towns they played were never the same again. "There's enough stories in that tour to fill a book...," he said, "Hank and I did shows together. We'd flip a coin to see who would go first..... I forget where we were at the time, but one day Hank said, 'Someday, when you slow down, you need to join the Opry.'" Of course, Lefty did, but his career was brief. It peaked for a four-year period between 1950 and 1954, when he scored five number one country hits and a further ten top ten entries. Lefty's first Top 10 hit in years, "The Long Black Veil" in 1959, was in my opinion, his best. In 2019, it was selected by the US Library of Congress for preservation in the National Recording Registry for being "culturally, historically, or aesthetically significant." His drinking and lack of good management left him with many hitless years, and he died on July 19, 1975, of a massive stroke, due in part to his alcoholism. He was only 47.

A song written by **Faron Young,** another honky tonk singer, might apply to his own life, as well as Williams' and Lefty's. "Live Fast, Love Hard, Die Young" was Faron's first number-one song and his fifth consecutive top ten hit. It spent three weeks at the top of the Billboard Country Music Chart in 1955.

He was born and raised in Shreveport where seeing Hank Williams perform on the Louisiana Hayride changed his interest from pop to country music. Webb Pierce, who befriended him and brought him on the Louisiana Hayride in 1951. There's another connection with another County star. Faron was dating a young lady named Billie Jean Jones. Hank Williams arranged a double date and then moved in on Faron's date at gunpoint. Billie Jean became the second Mrs. Hank Williams.

He had a role as a sheriff in the movie *Hidden Guns,* which earned him the nickname of The Singing Sheriff. Another country star, Roger Miller, got his start playing in Faron's band, Country Deputies. Faron's biggest hit, "Hello Walls," gained him a pop following.

By the '70s, his drinking was getting him into more trouble. He was known to say, "I am not an alcoholic, I'm a drunk," He got arrested over incidents where he attacked members of his audiences and on one occasion, he shot out the lights in a Nashville bar.

Faron Young ended his own life with a gunshot in December 1996.

Webb Pierce is another Louisiana-born honky tonker, born in Monroe on August 8, 1921, and influenced by a mix of Jimmy Rodgers, Gene Autry, and Cajun bands. He joined Louisiana Hayride in its first year, 1948. His early band includes several players who later achieved stardom on their own, pianist Floyd Cramer, guitarist-vocalist Faron Young, and vocalists Teddy and Doyle Wilburn who later performed as The Wilburn Brothers. His biggest hits were "There Stands the Glass," "Slowly," "More and More," "Back Street Affair," "Why Baby Why," and "In the Jail House Now." Other hits included "Oh, So Many Years" and "Finally" which were duets with Kitty Wells.

He had spots in several movies, but he is best remembered for his lavish lifestyle. His costumes were designed by Nudie Cohen, who also decorated Webb's two convertibles with silver dollars. Webb offered tours of his opulent home with its $30,000 guitar-shaped swimming pool until his neighbors, led by another famous singer Ray Stevens, filed suit and ended the tours as a neighborhood disturbance. Like many other honky tonk singers, he was fond of alcohol and died of pancreatic cancer on February 24, 1991.

Don Gibson wrote at least three of the most famous songs in country music history. Born Donald Eugene Gibson in Shelby, North Carolina, he began playing with a local band, Sons of the Soil, on a Shelby radio station, WOHS. His biggest talent was songwriting. His "Sweet Dreams" helped make Patsy Cline a star. It was his first big hit and won him a contract with Acuff-Rose Publications and a recording deal with MGM. His two other most famous songs were written on the same day: "Oh Lonesome Me" and "I Can't Stop Loving You." "I Can't Stop Loving You" was recorded over 700 times in many music genres and sold over thirty million records worldwide.

His hometown of Shelby honored him by transforming The State Theater, built in 1939, as the Don Gibson Theatre. It's a combination museum about Don Gibson, and a venue for music and an occasional comedy act plus special summer movie series. In the lobby, there are guitars, photos, and artifacts from Gibson's career. Backstage, many artists who performed there signed the wall. There are autographs of Chubby Checker, Vince Gill, Travis Tritt, and many others.

Around town there are hand-painted disks of his music featuring one of his hits where visitors can hear a sample of the song. One wall of a local boutique features a mural of Don Gibson. It's part of the North Carolina Musician Murals across the state.

Country Music Hall of Fame Museum honors those who made big contributions to Country Music. Every country singer is there from

Minnie Pearl and Roy Acuff to Brooks and Dunn and The Judds. You'll find every type of country music from early hillbilly to outlaw to southern rock. The museum is huge and so are some artifacts. There's Elvis's gold-plated Cadillac. Webb Pierce's '62 Bonneville Convertible Nudie Mobile, designed by Nashville's most flashy clothing designer-to-the-stars. It has steer horns on the front bumper, a bucking bronco, and a colt revolver on the hood, six shooters for door handles, a gun on the trunk, and a saddle between the bucket seats.

It's not just singers. Songwriter team Felice and Boudleaux Bryant, best known for their hit "Rocky Top," the state song of Tennessee, has an exhibit.

Chet Atkins later became known as "Mr. Guitar" and "The Country Gentleman." He, along with Owen Bradley and Bob Ferguson, are credited with creating the Nashville sound, a style which increased country music's appeal to pop audiences. He produced and managed of RCA Victor's Nashville studios, was responsible for building of the legendary RCA Studio B, the first real recording studio built on Music Row and later the creation of studio B's adjacent building RCA Studio A. He managed and produced for the biggest of big names, and in the midst of the riots and turmoil of the 1960s Civil Rights Movement, he signed the company's first African American singer, Charley Pride.

With Nashville being the home of country music, there had to be recording studios. Historic RCA Studio B is Music City's only studio tour. You board a bus at the Country Music Hall of Fame Museum, which also owns Studio B, and a guide tells you the history as you drive to Music Row to see for yourself. The tours are limited in the number of guests and must get booked ahead to be sure of a spot.

When you enter, there is a timeline showing who recorded what hits when and a plaque dedicated to Elvis. The studio has mikes, recording boards, instruments, and an isolation booth. It opened in 1957 and is considered the home of "The Nashville Sound," that changed country music from the raw honky-tonk sounds with a heavy fiddle and banjo, to more smooth string music with intricate background vocals.

What makes this place so special is who recorded in this studio. You feel if you are standing on sacred ground if you are a county or rock fan. Chet Atkins managed the studio and performed with many of the singers, including Elvis Presley. Elvis cut over 200 records here. Some other big names that held these mikes are Eddy Arnold, Waylon Jennings, Bobby Bare, Dolly Parton, Jim Reeves, Willie Nelson, Mickey Gilley, Charley Pride, and the Everly Brothers. That's just a start.

The singers get all the recognition, but the people who create the songs deserve credit. They get it at The Musicians Hall of Fame. All genres get representation here. When you enter, the sign says "From Edison to Ipod." There is a big exhibit with a piano showing the RCA dog sitting on it in front of the words, "God bless the boys who make the noise on 16th Avenue." From the early members of the Grand Old Opry to the UK singers who created the British Invasion, you'll see them all here.

The places that made music like Hitsville, USA, AKA Motown in Detroit, Sun Studio and Stax in Memphis, FAME and Muscle Shoals Studio in Alabama are well-represented. It is worth the time and money.

Jimmy Buffett defies description when it comes to genre. His music is country, rock, folk, calypso, and pop with coastal and tropical lyrics combined into gulf and western. He called his music "drunken Caribbean rock 'n' roll." His biggest rankings are on country charts.

He was born on Christmas day 1946 in Pascagoula, Mississippi and raised in Mobile and Fairhope, Alabama. He attended college at the University of Southern Mississippi in Hattiesburg, where he began playing guitar. After graduating in 1969, he moved to New Orleans and played on the street and at what was then Bayou Room nightclub on Bourbon Street. He moved to Nashville in 1970, and recorded his first album, *Down to Earth,* a combination country/folk rock. It went nowhere, but he did get a job at a Nashville club.

His friend and fellow country singer, Jerry Jeff Walker, invite him to his home in Coconut Grove. From there they would drive to Key West and play on the streets. Buffett loved the laid back atmosphere and moved there where he would play for drinks at the Chart Room Bar in the Pier House Motel.

His album, *Changes in Latitudes, Changes in Attitudes,* featuring his breakthrough hit song "Margaritaville" in 1977, assured his place in musical history. His duo with Alan Jackson, "It's Five O'Clock Somewhere," was another chart topper.

He passed away on September 1, 2023, from a rare type of skin cancer. His music, best-seller books, and his successful business ventures with Margaritaville Hotels and Casinos keep his memory alive.

The Everly Brothers, Don and Phil, came by their musical talent naturally. They performed as children with their parents, Ike and Margaret Everly as "The Everly Family" in the 1940s. While they were still in West High School in Knoxville, Tennessee, the brothers performed on Cas Walker's Farm and Home Hour, a popular Knoxville show. The found fame as the Everly Brothers when Chet Atkins liked their sound and got them a contract with Columbia. Their first hit song came in 1957, with "Bye Bye Love." Their music was between county and rock and roll, a melodious rockabilly sound.

They had future success with several hits including "Wake Up Little Susie," which was banned by many stations because of the question, "What was Susie and her boyfriend doing that they flell asleep after?" Being banned usually insured that a song became a hit.

The duo's career crashed and burned in 1973 when Don arrived for a show in Knott's Berry Farm in California drunk. He couldn't remember the lyrics of "Cathy's Clown," their latest hit. He and Phil began arguing on stage. The crowd was booing. Phil threw down his guitar, smashed it, and walked off. Don performed solo the next night, commenting to the audience "The Everly Brothers died ten years ago." Thus began a bitter ten-year separation.

They attempted solo careers but never achieved the level of success the duo had. They reunited in 1983 but with little success. They have a marker on Knoxville's Cradle of Music Tour.

(Top) Exhibit at Birthplace of Country Music in Bristol about the sessions
(Bottom) Band onstage at Carter Family Fold

(Top) Hank Williams statue in Montgomery
(Bottom) Hank's Cadillac at Hank Williams Museum in Montgomery

Lum York standing by Kawliga at Hank Williams Museum in Montgomery

(Top) Jimmie Rogers Museum in Meridian, MS
(Bottom) Don Gibson instruments and other artifacts at Don Gibson Theatre

(Top) Roy Acuff fiddle at the Museum of East Tennessee History in Knoxville
(Bottom) Exhibit at Glen Campbell Museum in Nashville

*(Top) Bronze of Minnie Pearl and Roy Acuff at Ryman Auditorium, Nashville
(Bottom) Country Music Hall of Fame in Nashville*

(Top) Studio B in Nashville (Bottom) Webb Pierce's Nudie Mobile in Country Music Hall of Fame, Nashville

(Top) Musicians Hall of Fame in Nashville
(Bottom) Alabama Music Hall of Fame in Tuscumbia, Alabama

Chapter 11 Western Music

In the late 1920s, cowboy music became popular. It paved the way for the later name change from "hillbilly music" to "country and western music." These singing cowboys stand out for me in that era.

In the fall of 1928, **Gene Autry** went to New York and auditioned for the Victor Talking Machine Company. He got rejected and was advised to copy Jimmie Rogers' yodeling style. Gene got a gig singing on Tulsa radio station KVOO billed as "Oklahoma's Yodeling Cowboy" in 1928. He got a recording deal with Columbia Records in 1929 and played on the highly popular Chicago National Barn Dance on WLS-AM radio. During this period he recorded covers of several different genre songs such as "The Death of Mother Jones" about labor unions, "Do Right, Daddy Blues," and "Black Bottom Blues," related to prohibition, but his first big hit was a song he co-wrote and recorded with Jimmy Long called "That Silver-Haired Daddy of Mine."

Gene made 640 recordings including the Christmas classics "Rudolph, The Red Nosed Reindeer," and "Frosty the Snowman." He wrote "Here Comes Santa Claus." His records sold over a 100 million copies, and he was the first singer to have a certified gold record. Over his lifetime, he accumulated more than a dozen gold and platinum records. His upward spiral vaulted him to becoming a Hollywood cowboy star and eventually one of the richest men in America. He is best known for the Ray Whitley composition "Back in the Saddle Again."

The next singing cowboy began life named Leonard Franklin Slye. He grew up singing with his family on their farm and learned to yodel to communicate with his mother across long distances. By 1930 when he was 19 he and his family had moved to Inglewood, California from Ohio. The depression hit California as hard as Ohio and when the construction company he was working for went bust, he picked crops and lived in labor camps.

He began his singing career with Midnight Frolic radio program, on station KMCS in Inglewood where he played guitar, sang, and yodeled. He caught the attention of a local country music group, the Rocky Mountaineers, and joined them in August 1931. His next band adventure was with a group called O-Bar-O Cowboys based in Lubbock, Texas, where they played for dances and small theaters in the area. When the O-Bar-O Cowboys disbanded Roy and his fellow musicians, Bob Nolan and Tim Spencer, formed the Sons of the Pioneers in 1934. They signed a recording contract with the newly founded Decca label and had their first session on August 8, 1934, recording songs including "Tumbling Tumbleweeds."

In 1938, when Gene Autry was demanding more money, Republic Pictures hired Slye. First thing the studio did was change his name to **Roy Rogers**. He soon rivaled Gene Autry in popularity. Sons of the Pioneers continued as a group until the present day. Roy frequently sang with them, And they were often featured in his movies. His theme song, "Happy Trails to You," was written by his third wife, Dale Evans, who often co-stated in films with him.

Woodward Maurice Ritter was not a marketable name for a singing cowboy, either. Since he was born in Murvaul, Texas near Beaumont, on January 12, 1905, he used the nickname Tex. **Tex Ritter** began his career in 1928, singing mostly cowboy songs on KPRC-AM in Houston. That same year, he moved to New York City and was cast in the men's chorus of the Broadway show *The New Moon*. He moved up and was cast as Cord Elam in the Broadway production of *Green Grow the Lilacs* in 1931. This play was the original of the musical *Oklahoma*. He was cast in several other Broadway plays.

In 1932, he landed the starring role in New York City's first broadcast Western, *The Lone Star Ranger* on WOR-AM Radio. He later performed on the radio show, WHN *Barndance*.

In 1936, he made his movie debut in *Song of the Gringo* and continued to appear in 70 movies. He sang his "The Ballad of High Noon" for the movie, *High Noon*, and sang in person at 1952's Academy Awards ceremony, where it won Best Original Song.

Tex Ritter was the first artist signed with the newly formed Capitol Records. His "I'm Wastin' My Tears on You" ranked number one on the country chart and number 11 on the pop chart. Best remembered for his 1961 hit "I Dreamed of a Hillbilly Heaven," where he meets many of the deceased country music stars. Most of the song is spoken in his unique Texas accent, with him strumming his guitar for the background. After greeting Jimmie Rogers, Hank Williams, and other greats, Tex asks his host who else was expected in the next hundred years. The host hands him a book and Tex begins reading the names. He reads through Red Foley, Ernest Tubb, Gene Autry, Roy Acuff, Eddy Arnold, Tennessee Ernie, Jimmy Dean, Andy Griffith, Roy Rogers, and when he reads Tex Ritter, he pauses and says that he then woke up. The song was written by Eddie Dean, another Western singer and actor, but it will always be associated with Tex Ritter.

He was one of the founding members of the Country Music Association in Nashville, Tennessee, and helped in raising funds to build the Country Music Hall of Fame and Museum, which inducted him in 1964. He earned membership in the Grand Ole Opry in 1970. Early western singers are the ones that brought Nudie to the forefront as a costume designer for the stars. Particularly Roy Rogers, who loved children and wanted to be sure the children could see him when he was performing at large outdoor events like rodeos. They began the fad of adding bling to their costumes. Soon, almost all Nashville stars used Nudie.

A man who co-starred with Tex Ritter in the 1940 movie, *Take Me Back to Oklahoma,* was the person who made the biggest contribution to the Western sound, **Bob Wills** with his Texas Playboys. The style was used in Hollywood western films and was a mix of country, old-time, dixieland jazz, blues, and swing, a real merging of American music with a dash of polka added. It was called western swing.

Bob Wills was born on a cotton farm in Kosse, Texas, in 1905 to a family of musicians. He learned to play the fiddle and the mandolin early. Growing up on a cotton farm, most of his playmates were the Black children of the cotton pickers. From those families, he developed a love for the blues and field songs. At 16 Bob ran away from home and drifted, playing in minstrels and medicine shows. He went to barbering school and was able to get a job doing that when he got married, but he still continued with switching between several different bands.

When he relocated to Waco, Texas, after forming a new band, The Playboys, he gained enough popularity to aim for a bigger market. The band headed for Oklahoma City in January 1934 and, with his renamed Texas Playboys, Bob began broadcasting a daytime show over the 50,000-watt KVOO radio station. They played dances in the evenings. Bob mostly sang numbers like "One Star Rag," "Take Me Back to Tulsa," "Basin Street Blues," and "Steel Guitar Rag."

It was when he added a trumpet to the band after he hired Everet Stover as an announcer, then finding out that Stover had played with the New Orleans Symphony and directed the Texas governor's band in Austin. Wills had Stover begin playing trumpet with the band. With some misgivings, Wills hired saxophonist Zeb McNally and Smoky Dacus as a drummer.

Bob Wills wasn't the first musician to use this kind of dance music. One of his former bandmates, Milton Brown, had created a similar band but never achieved the success Wills did. Bob Wills was named "King of Western Swing."

WIlls and the Texas Playboys made their first commercial record in September 1935, in Dallas. His 1940 hit, "New San Antonio Rose" sold a million records and became the band's signature song.

The band began their first cross-country tour in November 1944. They played the Grand Ole Opry on December 30, 1944, and appeared on the Louisiana Hayride on KWKH, broadcasting from the Municipal Auditorium in Shreveport, Louisiana on April 3, 1948. By this time, his band was outperforming, both in attendance numbers and money earned, most of the big bands. Wills became wealthy. He lived a lavish lifestyle and was married five times, six if you count his marriage, divorce, re-marriage, and re-divorce within a one-year period to Mary Helen Brown, the widow of his former bandmate and other Texas swing bandleader, Milton Brown.

Even though he was inducted into the Country Music Hall of Fame in 1968, his fame and wealth had diminished. He dissolved the band in 1965. He was almost penniless after he ended up owing a lot of back taxes to the IRS. However, over the years, his music had been covered by many big name singers. One of his 1949 hits, "Ida Red Likes the Boogie," was adapted to one of the top rock and roll hits of 1955. It originally was adapted from a traditional song Wills had probably heard as a young boy.

Marty Robbins was best known for his cowboy songs like "Running Gun," "Big Iron," and "El Paso." He was also a talented songwriter, actor, and race car driver. He was born in Glendale, Arizona, on September 26, 1925, and died in Nashville on December 8, 1982.

Robbins began singing more of a pop or rock style in the early 1950s "White Sport Coat and a Pink Carnation" and "Don't Worry." He quickly became popular for his Western style country music artists. His unique baritone voice and his ability to tell stories through his songs like "El Paso", a 1959 ballad about a cowboy who avenges the death of his lover. It topped the country and pop charts and has been covered by many other artists.

Robbins wrote most of his own songs, including "Big Iron," "The Story of the Streets," and "Singing the Blues." Over the course of his career, he wrote more than 500 songs.

Robbins was inducted into the Country Music Hall of Fame in 1982, just two months before his death from heart disease. He was also inducted into the Nashville Songwriters Hall of Fame in 1975.

Kenny Rogers was born on August 21, 1938, in Houston, Texas He was a country music singer, songwriter, actor, and entrepreneur. Best known for "The Gambler." which almost became his alter-ego, but he initially pursued a career in jazz. He played bass and sang in a jazz trio called The Bobby Doyle Three when he was a student at the University of Texas. He dropped out to pursue a music career.

Some of his most famous songs besides "The Gambler" are "Lucille," "Coward of the County," and "Islands in the Stream," a duet with Dolly Parton. Rogers' smooth voice and storytelling ability won him many awards in country music. He won three Grammys and was inducted into the Country Music Hall of Fame in 2013.

In addition to a music career, Kenny Rogers also ventured into acting and appeared in several movies and TV shows. His most well-known was *The Gambler* TV movie series. He died on March 20, 2020.

Tex Ritter's costumes and artifacts at Tex Ritter Historical Park and Dutch Windmill Museum

Chapter 12 Women in Country Music

Until the early 1950s, women were mostly backup singers or did duets with male stars. Then things began to change. Several female singers proved they could be superstars in their own right.

Kitty Wells was country's first female superstar, nicknamed the "Queen of Country Music." Kitty Wells' journey to musical royalty was convoluted. She was born Ellen Muriel Deason on August 30, 1919, in Nashville and began singing with her sisters as the Deason Sisters as a teenager.

She married Johnny Wright and began singing with him and his sister as Johnny Right and the Harmony Girls. Kitty took her stage name from a folk song called "Sweet Kitty Wells." She toured with Johnny and Jack as a backup singer. In those days, women were usually considered the "girl singer" or the "backup singer."

When Kitty recorded the song "It Wasn't God who Made Honky Tonk Angels" in 1952 as an answering song to Hank Thompson's "The Wild Side of Life," she achieved stardom in her own right.

"It Wasn't God who Made Honky Tonk Angels," was banned from many stations and the Opry wouldn't play it, because it took on the double standard when it questioned that it was not God, but unfaithful husbands ignoring marriage vows, that created "Honky Tonk Angels." This was the first single by a female singer to peak at #1 in the history of the country music chart, which had only been out eight years, so it didn't include earlier female singers. The song crossed over to the pop charts as well.

Kitty followed up "Honky Tonk Angels" with a response to Webb Pierce's "Backstreet Affair" with another "answer" song called "Paying for that Backstreet Affair" that hit #6 on country charts. In 1956, Kitty became the first country female country singer to have an album recorded, "Kitty Wells Country Hit Parade." Her duet with Webb Pierce, "Finally," in 1964 was another of her many top ten hits.

Kitty Wells was the first female country star with her own syndicated television show along with her husband in 1969, The Kitty Wells/ Johnny Wright Family Show.

A perfect example of different genre's merging in music is a 1974 album called "Forever Young" she recorded for Capricorn Records, backed by members of The Allman Brothers and the Marshall Tucker bands (you'll learn more about Capricorn and the Allman Brothers in the Southern Rock chapter) In 1993, she collaborated with Dolly Parton, Loretta Lynn, and Tammy Wynette on an album called "Honky Tonk Angels." She died on July 16, 2012.

Patsy Cline was born Virginia Patterson Hensley on September 8, 1932. She is another country music star that broke many traditions and became a role model for female singers.

Patsy Cline was the first woman admitted to the country music Hall of Fame. Women in country music dressed in demure ladylike dresses in her time. Patsy wore cowgirl outfits and boots. Men might be able to keep their careers after a divorce, but not women. Patsy wasn't putting up with a bad marriage; she divorced her first husband, remarried, and still rose to stardom. She survived a near-fatal car crash and was back on stage performing at the Opry on crutches within the year. The main thing women didn't do in her time was become the star. Just as with Kitty Wells, men were the lead vocalist, women did back up or duets. Not Patsy. Not only did she get top billing, she had top songs. She was one of the first country artists to gain fame as a crossover singer in Pop. Her "I Fall to Pieces," recorded in 1961, crossed over to the Billboard Pop at number 12.

She scored a repeat country music number one with "She's Got You" which also hit the pop charts as number 14. Her 1962 hit, "Crazy," written by Willie Nelson, reached number two on the country charts and after her death it has gone on to become the number one jukebox hit of all-time.

Patsy Cline was only 30 years old on March 5, 1963, when a plane crash ended her life. Two must-see places for Patsy Cline fans are her home in Winchester, Virginia and the Patsy Cline Museum in Nashville.

Her home in Winchester is now a museum that traces her rise to stardom. This was Patsy's home longer than any other place. She lived here from November 1948 through June 1957. It was originally a log house built in the mid-1800s. It's listed on the National Registry of Historic Places and Virginia Landmark Register.

Patsy got her first break when she performed on Winchester radio station, WINC. An upright piano similar to the one on which Patsy first learned to play sits in the living room. She played by ear as she never learned to read music.

There is a recording in the living room that the docent plays where Arthur Godfrey speaks with Hilda and then introduced Patsy. Fans will note the version of "Walking After Midnight" she sings on the recording is slightly different from the recorded version one usually hears. She could not take her actual band and the band that backed her up was more of a pop band than county. Godfrey's comments after her performance were drowned out by the applause.

The picture on the piano shows the cowboy outfit she planned to wear. When she got to New York, the show's producer took her shopping and bought her a cocktail dress to wear. An upright piano similar to the one on which Patsy first learned to play sits in the living room. She played by ear as she never learned to read music.

Patsy's mother, Hilda, was a seamstress and made Patsy's costumes. Throughout the simple home, you see the costumes made with love on her mother's old Singer machine. On the table in the dining room there is a notebook with sketches Patsy created of the costume designs she wanted. The sewing machine and ironing board are in that room for the better lighting.

The two red chairs in the kitchen are original to the house. The kitchen and bath were added in 1953 when they enclosed a back porch to make a kitchen and a small half bathroom was added. This was when they got running water in the house. Prior to that, there was an outhouse. Hilda originally cooked on a small wooden stove.

Upstairs, there is one big room. The entire family slept in the room. Her pants and coat are displayed here. Hilda also made doll clothes to supplement the family income.

The four-drawer dresser allowed one drawer each for her, her mom, her sister, and her brother.

Patsy is buried in nearby Shenandoah Memorial Park with her husband, Charlie Dick, who passed away in 2005. A plaque reads "Death Cannot Kill What Never Dies: Love." People put pennies on Patsy's grave because, as our guide Joyce McKay told us, "It's supposed to bring you luck." Nearby there is a bell tower that used to play music. It was erected in her honor by Loretta Lynn, Dottie West, and other musician friends.

The Patsy Cline Museum is upstairs over the Johnny Cash Museum. It tells her story; the heartbreaks and the triumphs. There's the key to New York City given by New York's mayor when Patsy Cline and Minnie Pearl were the only women in a Grand Old Opry Show featuring Nashville's biggest names at Carnegie Hall.

When Patsy's father deserted the family, Patsy went to work as a teen at the soda fountain of the neighborhood Gaunt's Drugstore. A replica of the booth and many artifacts from Gaunt's are on display.

Her career is showcased here. Several displays contain her records and albums. Costumes she wore at various performances are on display. Also, there are the costumes and posters of the movie made about her life, *Sweet Dreams*, starring Jessica Lang. There are artifacts displayed from her personal life including the many costume jewelry pieces Patsy loved, an old time clock radio, a hair dryer, her suitcase partially packed, an iron, and many of the everyday things any woman would have had in the '50s and '60s. When she began making money with her records, she purchased her dream home in Goodlettsville, Tennessee. The rec room and dining room are recreated here. She and Charley Dick lived there for less than a year before Patsy's death.

Patsy Cline was someone who never lost appreciation for her fans. She answered many of their letters, telling what was happening in her life and asking about theirs. Many of the letters are quite long, several pages. Her letters are on display and there is an interactive exhibit where you can read them all completely.

The most poignant display is of the plane crash that took the lives of Patsy Cline, Cowboy Copas, Hawkshaw Harkins and Randy Hughes, her manager who was piloting the plane on March 5th, 1963. Some of the items are her broken Elgin watch, telegrams and letters of condolence, newspaper headline stories of the crash. One item struck home about the personal toll of the tragedy, Patsy's mother's handkerchief she had at the funeral.

When you leave this museum, you will feel like you know the real Patsy Cline personally.

Loretta Lynn, born in Butcher Hollow, Kentucky, on April 14, 1932, had a career spanning six decades. Her music was a view into her own life. Her "Don't Come Home A-Drinkin' With Lovin' on Your Mind," and "You Ain't Woman Enough To Take My Man," reflected on her own cheating husband's affairs and alcoholism. Loretta's self-written "You Ain't Woman Enough" was the first number one hit written by a woman. Her 1971 number one hit, "Coal Miner's Daughter," was named among NPR's "100 Most Significant Songs of the 20th Century." It was made into a movie that garnered seven Academy Award nominations.

Her music often dealt with life for the average woman like "The Pill," telling that with the advent of birth control pills, women had more choices. It, along with her "Wings Upon Your Horns" which tells of a man rejecting a woman who gave him her virginity, and "Rated X," about the stigma of being a divorced woman in the 1900s, were banned on many country stations.

Loretta Lynn was the most awarded female country recording artist, and the only female ACM Artist of the Decade for 1970s. She won three Grammy Awards, seven American Music Awards, eight Broadcast Music Incorporated awards, 13 Academy of Country Music awards, eight Country Music Association, and 26 fan-voted Music City News awards. She was the first woman in country music to receive a certified gold album for 1967's "Don't Come Home a' Drinkin'." She piled up 24 Number one hit singles and 11 number one albums and toured on the road for 57 years. She wrote more than 160 songs and released 60 albums.

Loretta was fiercely loyal to her fans. One of my favorite memories of Loretta Lynn was when I attended a concert she gave in Hiawassee, Georgia, at Anderson Music Hall in the late 1990s, shortly after her husband died. My friend and I saw her entering and tried to get an autograph signed. She didn't have time as she had to get onstage, but promised to sign later. After a long show under hot lights, her escorts guided her back to her tour bus behind the hall. We were standing there and asked one of the guards to ask her to sign our programs. He said he would bring it to her, but she was very tired and overheated, so no promises. Sure enough, she signed both of them.

Loretta Lynn died in her sleep at her ranch in Hurricane Mills, Tennessee on October 4, 2022, at the age of 90. A star that burned bright in Country Music Heaven but never forgot her roots. I was excited to get the opportunity to see for myself, close up and in person, the land and the people that molded a *Coal Miner's Daughter* into the Queen of Country Music.

I visited her home several years ago. Loretta's brother, Herman Webb, gave the tour then and told a few antidotes about the hardscrabble existence of the Webb family. Now, you will meet some other member of the family when you take the tour. Herman passed away in 2018.

The cabin is tiny, especially when you realize there were eight children in the Webb family. It's small and dark but when you look at all the pictures, you see what Loretta meant when she sang, that they were poor, but had love. Sure enough, the "well where she drew water" is still in the front yard. I will never forget the moment when I touched that same well.

I asked Herman when the family realized that Loretta had a special talent. He replied, "We all sang. Shoot, she was just one more kid with a loud mouth around here."

Herman took us through the house and then brought us back to his modest general store for a moon pie and old-fashioned soft drink. Loretta's niece, Sarah McCoart, sang "Coal Miner's Daughter" for us. Although she was not yet in her teens, she had already performed with her famous aunt. Musical talent runs in that family.

We also got a good look at a miner's life. The tiny entrance to the mine where Loretta's dad shoveled coal to earn a poor man's dollar. It was not a vocation I would want to pursue, but millions of hard-working men still mine, much the same as it was done a generation ago. Unions have improved their life somewhat, but it's easy to see why the life of a singer looked so good to Loretta,

Crystal, and lots of Kentucky men and women who followed Kentucky's Music Highway into Nashville.

Contrary to popular opinion, Butcher Holler is not a town: it's an area located just outside the hamlet of Van Lear. Van Lear was established by the Consolidation Coal Company and named for one of the directors, Mr. Van Lear Black. The former country store is now the Van Lear Museum, telling about Loretta and Crystal, life in a mining town, complete with the doctor's office who delivered Loretta's babies, and a coal miner's life. Next door to the museum is the local hangout where Loretta and Mooney used to meet. Icky's has more 50s memorabilia than you ever saw in one place.

Today, tourism has replaced mining as Van Lear's top industry. Folks travel from all over to view the place made famous by movies and songs. Standing in that rustic cabin I realized this is not just an old home place, it's a shrine and its patron saint is a hardworking woman who used her talent to change "A Coal Miner's Daughter" into a legend in her own time.

Dolly Parton is a true one-of-a-kind artist. She was born January 19, 1946 in the Smokey Mountains of Tennessee and as of this writing is still going strong. Dolly has sold more than 100 million records worldwide, making her one of the best-selling female artists of all time. She has 44 Top 10 country albums so far, a record for any artist, and has 110 singles. She has written over 3,000 songs and received 11 Grammy Awards. Twenty-five of her singles reached no. 1 on the Billboard country music charts, which sets a record for a female artist. She is tied with Reba McEntire on that honor.

Dolly was inducted into the Country Music Hall of Fame, received the National Medal of Arts, and was inducted into the Rock and Roll Hall of Fame.

Her mother is of Welsh ancestry, so she introduced young Dolly to the folklore and ancient ballads brought to the mountains from the old homeland. She credits her mother for her music knowledge and her father for her business sense. Although he was poor and illiterate, Dolly claims he was the smartest man she knew.

Several of her songs tell of her family's poverty, most notably her "Coat of Many Colors" and "In the Good Old Days (When Times Were

Bad)." To escape the trap of poverty, she headed for Nashville the day after she graduated from high school. Her early success came from her songwriting. Teamed with her uncle, Bill Owens, she signed with Combine Publishing quickly and wrote several charting singles including two Top 10 hits in the mid 1960s, Bill Phillips's "Put It Off Until Tomorrow" and Skeeter Davis's "Fuel to the Flame." To date, she has written over 3,000 songs. As soon as her contract with Combine Music ended, she teamed with her Uncle Bill and started their own publishing company. They named it Owe-Par for parts of their last names. An extremely smart move, as so many stars wrote hit songs that made money for the publishing company and left them in the cold.

She teamed up with Porter Wagoner. (Yes, he should rate a mention if there were enough room.) In 1968, the Country Music Association named them Vocal Group of the Year. In February 1971, she had her first number-one single, "Joshua." "Coat of Many Colors" reached number four the same year. Seeking to find her own place in the music world, she split with Wagoner. It was somewhat contentious. She eventually bought out her contract with him in 1974. She wrote and dedicated "I Will Always Love You" to Wagoner. It went to number one on the country chart.

Dolly began having a strong influence on pop culture when many performers including, Olivia Newton-John, Emmylou Harris, Linda Ronstadt, and others, covered her songs. The most noteworthy was Whitney Houston's cover of "I will Always Love You."

Dolly appeared in several films. Her song "9 to 5," which was the theme song for the movie of the same name in which she starred with Jane Fonda and Lily Tomlin, hit number one on the country chart, the pop chart, and the adult-contemporary charts. Dolly Parton is still one of the few female country singers to have a number-one single on these three charts simultaneously. The song was a nominee for an Academy Award for Best Original Song.

Dolly received a second Academy Award nomination for Best Original Song in 2005 for "Travelin' Thru" written for the film *Transamerica* about a transgender woman. She's still going strong, and in 2020, released her movie *Christmas on the Square*.

Dolly has risen to the top as a businesswoman as well. She started her own publishing company shortly after arriving in Nashville, so she owns her entire catalog of music. Her company is worth about $150 million, according to Forbes. She owns eight restaurants and dinner theaters and is co-owner of a water park and spa. Her investments in her native East Tennessee, notably Dollywood in Pigeon Forge of which she is co-owner, have brought jobs and prosperity to her home state as well as reaching into other states.

Dollywood is more than a theme park. You can see how Dolly lived over the years there. Dolly's Tennessee Mountain Home has a two-room replica of her Locust Ridge childhood home. Or you can visit her now-retired touring bus and see how she lived on the road. Besides fun rides and attractions, you will find several theaters with live music acts.

Her latest venture is Doggie Parton, a dog clothing and accessories line. A portion of every purchase of Doggie Partin goes to support Willa B Farms, a rescue farm for domestic and farm animals in Old Hickory, Tennessee.

Dolly supported many charitable efforts as well, particularly in the area of literacy, with book giveaways to children. In 2003, her efforts to preserve the bald eagle with her eagle sanctuary at Dollywood, earned her the Partnership Award from the US Fish and Wildlife Service.

Dolly Parton has revealed that she invested her royalties from Whitney Houston's cover of "I Will Always Love You" into a Black community in Nashville. When Houston covered it in the 1992 romantic drama *"The Bodyguard"* it became a worldwide hit. According to Forbes, the song spent 14 weeks at the top of the US Billboard Hot 100 and earned Parton $10 million in royalties. Parton used the money she made to buy a "big office complex" in the "Black area of town" in honor of Houston, who died in 2012 at the age of 48.

With the spread of COVID in 2020, she donated $1 million to research at Vanderbilt University Medical Center for the development of the Moderna vaccine. Dolly was vaccinated against COVID-19 at Vanderbilt University and tweeted about it, "Dolly gets a dose of her own medicine." She even sang about it with a song set to the tune of her "Jolene." Instead of "Jolene," she inserted "Vaccine, vaccine,

vaccine, vaccine," and instead of begging Jolene not to take her man, she begs people to not hesitate about getting the vaccine because "once you're dead, it's too late."

On a whimsical note, a rescued alligator just about three feet found in a Sanford, Florida lake with much of its upper jaw cut off in September 2023, probably in a snare trap, was named "Jawlene" in honor of Dolly's hit song. It is no auburn-haired beauty, but it has found its new forever home at Gatorland, just south of Orlando. When park CEO Mark McHugh announced the name, picked from suggestions from the public, Gatorland's international ambassador, Savannah Boan, who held the 'gator, sang out: "Jawlene, Jawlene, Jawlene!" As of 2022, *Ledger Note* ranked her the wealthiest country music star in the country with a net worth of $675 million.

Tammy Wynette helped ensure a place for women as country music stars during her tumultuous career. She was born Virginia Wynette Pugh on May 5, 1942, near Tremont, Mississippi. Her voice fit the Nashville sound or countrypolitan style of country that became popular in the mid '50s. It veered away from the rougher honky tonk sound to a smoother, more pop style with crooning lead vocals backed by heavy use of string instruments and backing vocals.

Tammy Wynette's musical career was outstanding, but her personal life left her often "out standing in the rain." She had twenty singles that topped the Billboard country chart. Tammy sold an estimated 30 million records worldwide. She received two Grammy Awards, three Country Music Association awards, and two Academy of Country Music Awards. Wynette was also among country music's first female performers to have discs certify gold and platinum by the Recording Industry Association of America. Her influence as a country music artist led to several inductions into music associations, including the Country Music Hall of Fame and the Nashville Songwriters Hall of Fame.

Her best-known song, "Stand by Your Man," won both acclaim and criticism, especially when Hilary Clinton said she wouldn't "stand by my man like Tammy Wynette." about infamous Clinton–Lewinsky scandal.

Tammy's personal life took a bad turn when she married Euple Byrd at age 17. They had three children before the marriage went south in part due to Byrd's inability to hold a steady job. Wynette enrolled in cosmetology school as a way to help support her children and herself. When she divorced Byrd in 1965, she moved to Nashville, Tennessee, to pursue a country music career. While staying in a cheap motel, she met her second husband, Don Chapel, who was a desk clerk there while trying for a career as a songwriter. Chapel's best known song is "When The Grass Grows Over Me" sung by George Jones.

At the same time, Billy Sherrill heard Tammy sing, liked her voice, and got her signed with Epic Records. He suggested she use the name "Tammy Wynette." Her first single, "Apartment No. 9," was released in 1966 to only moderate success. In 1967, she had her first hit with "Your Good Girl's Gonna Go Bad." Her career went uphill from there. She had several number one Billboard country singles "I Don't Wanna Play House, D-I-V-O-R-C-E," and the infamous "Stand by Your Man." She and Billy Sherrill wrote it in just 15 minutes.

Meantime, her marriage with Chapel was on the rocks and in 1968, it came to a dramatic close when Chapel and Wynette had an argument while George Jones was visiting at dinner one night. She and Jones had toured together and had romantic feelings for one another. When the argument got heated, Jones threw over the dining room table and escorted Tammy and her three children out of the house. She and Jones married in February 1969.

As a duet, they were loved by their fans. They had several number one singles, including "We're Gonna Hold On" and "Golden Ring." They became known as "Mr. and Mrs. Country Music."

Their relationship was tumultuous. George Jones was quite attached to his bottle and became aggressive when drunk. How aggressive depends on which biography you read-they both wrote one. Tammy suggested that his youthful nickname "The Possum," because of his close-set eyes and facial features, might relate instead to his playing possum when drinking and pretending to be sleeping when he was really listening to the conversations around him. He would jump up and become aggressive when something was said he didn't like. They divorced in 1975. But sang and toured together several times after.

Tammy married husband number four, George Richey, in 1978. Her health deteriorated. She became addicted to prescription pills and died in 1998.

One female singer left her imprint on country music with a song that resounds today in women's right and political arguments. In **Bobby Gentry**'s "Ode to Billie Joe," The song's narrator, a young Mississippi girl, comes in from picking cotton to dinner and learns from her mother that Billie Joe McAllister committed suicide by jumping off the Tallahatchie Bridge. The girl is too upset to eat. The mother adds that the preacher thought he saw a girl resembling the narrator on Choctaw Ridge throwing something off the Tallahatchie Bridge earlier.

Years pass in the song, but the girl never recovers from what happened. The song ends with her as an older woman picking flowers and tossing them into the river by the bridge. It hints that she and Billie Joe were lovers, and she became pregnant. They threw the baby off the bridge since unwed mothers were not accepted in rural Mississippi with its overwhelming religious influence and abortion was unheard of there. Billie Joe could not live with his guilt, so he jumped off the same bridge. Today there is a marker on the Mississippi Country Music Trail marking the place where Billie Joe is supposed to have jumped.

Loretta Lynn's brother, Herman Webb, showing us some of Loretta's things at their birthplace

(Top) Patsy Cline's birthplace in Winchester, VA
(Bottom) Her grave in Winchester

Exhibit at Patsy Cline Museum in Nashville

Chapter 13 Bluegrass

Ralph Stanley's Mountain Music helped create what is today known as Bluegrass. The Ralph Stanley Museum in Clintwood, Virginia is an interactive musical journey through his career and the music that got its start in the mountains of southwest Virginia. Ralph and his brother Carter founded the Clinch Mountain Boys band in Norton, Va. He was awarded an honorary Doctor of Music from Lincoln Memorial University, a second honorary doctorate degree in music in 2014 from Yale University, and received the Living Legend Award from the Library of Congress and a National Medal of Arts. He was the first artist given the Traditional American Music Award by the National Endowment for the Humanities. President Bush awarded him the National Medal of Arts in 2006. Browsing through his museum gave me new insights into the beginnings of mountain music and how bluegrass was created from it. Dora Wallace, museum director, started us with a brief history of Dr. Stanley and then turned us loose to browse. There are displays of the major instruments used in Mountain Music, mandolins, banjos, guitars, and fiddles. The headsets let us listen to stories and songs through the museum, which does a wonderful job of telling not only Ralph Stanley's story but that of Mountain Music and Bluegrass.

The museum displays show how this original music of the mountain people learned in primitive churches merged into Country and even Pop. One placard shows the connection with musicians like Loretta Lynn and Chuck Berry's songs. The highlight of our visit was meeting and hearing Ralph Stanley's grandson, Nathan Stanley, sing a moving ballad about his grandfather, "He'll Always be Papaw to Me."

Dr. Stanley's fan base grew to include many who had never heard of him in 2000 when his music was featured in the film *O Brother, Where Art Thou?* His soulful recording of "O Death" won a Grammy for Best Male Country Vocal Performance. He won a second Grammy for "Lost in the Lonesome Pines," a bluegrass album a collaboration with Jim Lauderdale. Although Dr. Stanley's music fit the earliest bluegrass sound, he preferred to think of it as mountain music telling the stories of Appalachia. "Old-time mountain style, that's what I like to call it," he said in a 2001 interview.

When you're in Ralph Stanley country of southwestern Virginia, stop in at Axe Handle Distillery. They have Friday night community bluegrass picking sessions every Friday from spring to fall. Anyone can bring an instrument and join in. They also have events with local musicians. When we visited, Tim White, a well-known bluegrass musician and host of the PBS television concert series, *Song of the Mountains*, entertained us.

Bill Monroe is considered the "Father of Bluegrass Music." Monroe's instrument of choice was a mandolin, but as a teen, he played guitar with his Uncle Pen at local dances. There he met Arnold Schulz, a black musician who played a bluesy kind of guitar and fiddle using a "thumb style" or "Travis picking" style. Bill Monroe later played with Schultz at dances. This is probably where the blues merged into his style. He started his adult career teaming with his brothers, Birch and Charlie, as The Monroe Brothers. They played square dance songs, traditional music and gospel numbers. In 1932, they were touring with WLS Touring Company Barn Dance as dancers, appearing with the Hoosier Hot Shots and Red Foley.

In 1938, Bill split and started his own band, The Blue Grass Boys, named from the area of Kentucky where he was born. With this new band, Bill built upon his earlier innovations, an edgier music with touches of what later became country blended in. He began recording again with RCA. By the 1940s, Bluegrass, as we know it today, began with his band, now consisted of Earl Scruggs, Lester Flatt, Chubby Wise, and Joel Price, who all became respected names in the music field. Scruggs' three finger picking style changed the banjo from a background instrument to the forefront. They were members of the Grand Ole Opry. While playing together, they recorded "Blue Moon of Kentucky" which was added to the National Recording Registry, by the Library of Congress and later enshrined in the Grammy Hall of Fame. You may recall it was the first song recorded by Elvis; some credit it with being the start of rock and roll.

Lester Flatt and **Earl Scruggs** left the Bluegrass Boys and began their own band in 1949. It sparked a twenty-plus year feud with Monroe. They called their backup band, the Foggy Mountain Boys. Flatt and Scruggs changed bluegrass even more when they added the Dobro, played by Burkett "Uncle

Josh" Graves, to their band. They brought bluegrass into mainstream popularity in the early 1960s with their theme song for the television sitcom, *The Beverly Hillbillies*, "The Ballad of Jed Clampett." Added to their success, their "Foggy Mountain Breakdown" was featured in the 1967 film *Bonnie and Clyde*. They became the most commercially successful bluegrass band of their time. "Foggy Mountain Breakdown," originally released in 1949, won two Grammy Awards and, in 2005, was selected by the Library of Congress' National Recording Registry as one of its "works of unusual merit."

The city of Shelby, North Carolina recognizes one of its musical legends in a big way. The former Cleveland County Courthouse, built around 1907, is now Earl Scruggs Center honoring native son, Earl Scruggs, who perfected the three-fingered style of banjo picking. Watch the video about Earl Scruggs' life, then check out the rest of the museum. Earl Scruggs' sculpture is so lifelike you think he's going to swing that banjo around and start picking. The museum takes you through his career and that of his sons. Earl played with their band for many years after he and Lester Flatt dissolved their partnership.

The Center isn't just about Earl Scruggs. It has exhibits about the rise of the banjo from its African roots to its place in bluegrass and country music. There's a room where you can play one of the many instruments there.

Hazel Dickens, born June 1, 1925, carved West Virginia a piece of the Bluegrass pie. With Alice Gerrard, Dickens was one of the first women to record an album in the male dominated bluegrass genre. Her songs were about the hard life of miners. Not only did she record songs including "Black Lung," "Cold Blooded Murder," "Clay County Miner," and "Mannington Mine Disaster," she stood in picket lines for better working conditions for miners. She was a strong environmentalist. Her version of "Who's That Knocking," with Alice Gerrard for Folkways in 1965, is considered one of the earliest bluegrass records made by women. She appeared in the movie, *Matewan*, where she sang "Hills of Galilee," and *"Songcatcher."* She often sang at union rallies and benefits for mine workers. Her music was one of the earlier types of protest song. In 1994, Dickens became the first woman to receive the International Bluegrass Music Association's Merit Award. She was later inducted into the organization's Hall of Honor. She received a National Heritage Fellowship from the National Endowment for the Arts in 2001.

(Top) Sculpture of Earl Scruggs at Earl Scruggs Center in Shelby, SC
(Bottom) Exhibit at The Ralph Stanley Museum in Clintwood, Virginia

Chapter 14 The Outlaw movement

There were many who felt changing the country music style to a more pop sound was wrong. They created what came to be known as the Outlaw Movement. It was a sub-genre that brought back elements of the blues, folk, and honky tonk to country music.

One group, The Highwaymen, more than any other defined the movement. Some of the earliest to break with Nashville and begin playing this kind of music included Waylon Jennings, Willie Nelson, Johnny Cash, and Kris Kristofferson. They called themselves The Highwaymen after a popular song by that name they recorded.

The Highwaymen personified the sub-genre known as outlaw music. The Outlaws rebelled not only against Nashville's dictating every part of their music, but their style of dress and acceptable behavior. Outlaws made a point of letting their hair grow long, dressing in jeans, and often cowboy dress. They publicly admitted to smoking marijuana. They flaunted their disrespect for Nashville's polished image.

Waylon Jennings song, "Ladies Love Outlaws" released in 1972 on an album by the same name, is credited as being the first "Outlaw" song.

Waylon was always a rebel. He left high school at 16 because of his many disciplinary actions. He began performing on air in 1956 for local Texas station KVOW. As a DJ, his show was a mix of early rock and roll and country. At that time, white musicians like Pat Boone were doing cover songs of Black rock and rollers. Segregation in music was still strong. The station owner fired Jennings for playing two Little Richard records in a row. Next, Waylon began playing with Buddy Holly's band and was haunted by the memory of the plane crash that he felt should have killed him instead of the Big Bopper to whom Waylon had given his seat.

In the early 1960s, Waylon was living in Arizona and playing in a club around Phoenix, when Chet Atkins offered him a contract with RCA. His friend, Willie Nelson, who knew how Nashville worked, suggested he stay in Phoenix. But who ever listens to advice?

In 1966, Waylon released his early RCA albums, *Folk-Country*, followed by *Leavin' Town* and *Nashville Rebel*. *Leavin' Town*'s first two singles "Anita, You're Dreaming" and "Time to Burm Again" both hit Billboard's Hot Country chart at number 17. His third single from that album, a cover of Gordon Lightfoot's "(That's What You Get) For Lovin' Me," reached no. 9. His top 10 single, "Nashville Rebel," was used as the soundtrack to an independent film of the same name starring Waylon.

While he was living in Nashville, he met and shared an apartment with Johnny Cash. The same booking agency, Moeller Talent, Inc. managed both singers. Touring for 300 days a year on the road, the tours were often distant and close in time, so it made a hectic schedule. He couldn't play his own guitar or chose his own material to record. Waylon's ever present rebel began taking amphetamines.

In 1972, after Waylon's highly successful album, *Ladies Love Outlaws*, his recording contract ended. He was fed up with Nashville and hired Neil Reshen as his new manager. Reshen negotiate a new contract with RCA, getting Waylon a $75,000 advance and complete artistic control. His inner outlaw now had free rein.

Wanted! The Outlaws, was an album by Waylon Jennings, Waylon's wife Jessi Colter, Willie Nelson, and Tompall Glaser, on the RCA label. It included some previously released songs mixed with four new songs, and was recorded to capitalize on the new outlaw country movement in 1976. *Wanted! The Outlaws* became the first country album to be platinum-certified, reaching sales of one million.

It was just the beginning of the success the Outlaw Movement brought to Waylon. "This Time" and "I'm a Ramblin' Man" topped the charts in 1974. In 1975 "Dreaming My Dreams," "Luckenbach, Texas (Back to the Basics of Love)," and "Are You Sure Hank Done It This Way," charted at number one. "Are You Sure Hank Done It This Way" became Waylon's first album to be certified gold in 1978.

However, Waylon's drug habit made the outlaw image a bit too real. Perhaps his being almost arrested by drug enforcement because of a cocaine package he received had something to do with it.

He made his feelings clear in the song "Don't You Think This Outlaw Bit's Done Got Out of Hand?" Due to copyright issues, I can't quote exactly, but to paraphrase Waylon as he tells the story in the second verse of the song, we were so wrapped up recording the music we never saw the front room full of officers of the law until they came into the studio while Waylon and the boys were in the middle of a song and arrested him for something that was already long gone.

There's a lot more to the story. Waylon was always fond of kids and had planned a trip to Jamaica for a little girl with brain cancer. His manager, Neil Reshen in New York, had made mistakes and not gotten the trip booked correctly. As an apology, Reshen sent Waylon a gift of an ounce of cocaine using a special delivery company. Probably Mark Rothbaum, Reshen's assistant, took the package to the delivery service.

The delivery serviceman got suspicious and called Drug Enforcement Agency (DEA) who removed most of the cocaine but left enough to incriminate Waylon. They then ordered the package delivered and got a warrant to search Waylon's office in Nashville. What messed the arrest up was that Waylon was next door to his office at a studio he rented, but did not own, finishing up his vocals on the song "Storms Never Last" for *New South* an album he was doing with Hank Williams, Jr.

Waylon's secretary, Lori Evans, picked the package up at the Nashville airport and brought it to the recording studio that was located next door to Waylon's office.

Lori handed Waylon the package, which he took into the studio. When he opened it and saw what was inside, he laid it aside and went back to recording. The DEA agents were confused when she didn't go to the office, but followed a short distance behind her. They burst into the control room, flashing the warrant and badges.

Waylon's drummer and close friend, Richie Albright, was the first person the DEA agents encountered. While he was speaking to the agents, Richie pressed the call button, letting Waylon hear what was happening.

Waylon tossed the package under the baseboard, where it was somewhat hidden. Meantime, the agents were waiting for a warrant to search the studio. Waylon and Hank Jr. pretended to keep working and Richie said he needed to adjust Waylon's mike. He went back to the studio and hid the package in his pants. Came out and went to the restroom and flushed the evidence down the toilet.

When the warrant arrived, they arrested Waylon and charged him with "conspiring to possess and possessing with intent to distribute cocaine." Each charge carried a maximum of fifteen years in prison and a fifteen-thousand-dollar fine.

With no evidence to back the charge and the messed up warrant, Waylon was appearing with Willie to a sold-out crowd at Nashville's Municipal Auditorium twelve hours later.

In the mid-1980s, Johnny Cash, Kris Kristofferson, Willie Nelson, and Waylon Jennings formed The Highwaymen. They recorded three major label albums: two on Columbia Records and one for Liberty Records. Their 1985 debut album's title song, "Highwayman," a Jimmy Webb ballad about reincarnation, gave them their name. The song became a number one hit.

In 1990, they created a second album, *Highwayman 2*, which reached number four on the country album chart. The group's final release in 1995 on Liberty was *The Road Goes on Forever*, which did not chart as high.

Today, a portion of Waylon's legacy is kept alive by his son, Shooter Jennings, and by Tommy Townsend, a Georgia musician and owner of Grandaddy Mimms Distilling Company in Blairsville, Georgia.

Tommy met Waylon as a youngster and reconnected again as a teenage aspiring musician. He cut a demo that Waylon liked. Tommy played with Waylon's Waymore's Outlaws for about 15 years.

Waylon and Jerry Bridges, his bass player, helped gather songs for Townsend and helped him produce an album. Jennings also sings on several tracks including "Southern Man," "If You Can't Stand the Heat," "Holes in My Boots," and "A Good Love Died Tonight," and plays guitar on "The Picker" and "Southern Man." The album's recording was done in two sessions with many years between. "Southern Man," the title song, and a few others were cut in 1988. The remaining songs, "Trouble with a Capital T," "Stompin' Ground" and some others were cut in the late 90s. Despite Waylon's collaboration, the album didn't find a real label home and had limited release. Not until recently, when Tommy signed a contract with Audium Nashville in September 2021, they learned about the album. They wanted *Southern Man* released.

I met Tommy Townsend in Blairsville while working on a story about a music road trip, but was mainly focusing on his distillery. I visited his Grandaddy Mimms Distilling Company, and he was kind enough to get me into the concert he was doing that evening with Waymore's Outlaws. Wow! Besides being a really nice guy, he even sounds a lot like Waylon.

I had the pleasure of seeing **Willie Nelson** in concert at the Saint Augustine Amphitheater. If I hadn't already been a big fan, I would have been after that concert.

Even if Willie had never recorded a song, he would be famous for the ones he wrote. "Crazy," recorded by Patsy Cline, "Hello Walls" by Faron Young, and "Night Life" covered by just about every singer out there including B. B. King, Ray Price, Doris Day, Dolly Parton, Aretha Franklin, and others in many different genres. Willie was recording then under contract for Pappy Daily of D Records who refused the song as "not country." In my opinion, Daily was right. "Night Life" is not country. Even its words, about listening to the blues they're playing, tell you it's a fantastic blues song. Willie sold the song for $150 to Paul Buskirk, a music school owner, in 1960 while working at a club in Houston.

Willie moved to Nashville in 1961 but couldn't find a label to sign him. After Patsy Cline's recording of "Crazy," he signed a contract with Liberty Records and later RCA, but had no singing success. In 1972, he moved back to Texas and considered resigning from the music business. But it was in Austin, with its younger Hippie population, that his career thrived. No longer bound by Nashville's conservative rules. He returned to recording, hired Neil Reshen. Remember that guy who got Waylon "in trouble with the man?" Reshen was also the man who would make Willie a real outlaw in trouble with the IRS by filing extensions and not paying taxes. After that fiasco, Willie dropped Reshen as manager in favor of Mark Rothbaum, Reshen's assistant who admitted to sending the cocaine.

Before those calamities, Willie's first Atlantic Recording album, *Shotgun Willie*, in May 1973, earned excellent reviews and his second, *Phases and Stages*, in 1974, included the hit single "Bloody Mary Morning." The same year, he produced and starred in the pilot episode of PBS *Austin City Limits,* the still-going, longest running music series in television history.

When he moved to Columbia Records, his contract gave him complete creative control. His first album in 1975 was *Red Headed Stranger*. Columbia was not happy about an album with basically a guitar, piano, and drums accompaniment to the vocals. Nelson's contract allowed its release. Willie's cover of Fred Rose's "Blue Eyes Crying in the Rain," released as a single shortly before the album, was Nelson's first number one hit as a singer. It rocked to the top of the Billboard chart for Top Country Albums and reached the 28th spot on its 43-week run in the Top LPs & Tapes chart. It was certified gold by the Recording Industry Association of America, on March 11, 1976, and on November 21, 1986, reached double-platinum status. The Red Headed Stranger became Willie's unofficial nickname. It also confirmed what any of his followers already knew; Willie Nelson was not just a country singer, he was a true outlaw.

After his successful collaboration on *Wanted, The Outlaws*, Willie released two more platinum albums in 1978, *Waylon & Willie*, another collaboration with Jennings that included "Mammas Don't Let Your Babies Grow Up to Be Cowboys", and *Stardust*, a mix of that old favorite jazz, pop, and folk, that went platinum the same year and stayed on the Billboard's Country Album charts for ten years. The following year, he won a Grammy Award for Best Male Country Vocal Performance for one song on that album, "Georgia on My Mind."

Willie has collaborated with almost every other singer, including, Julio Iglesias on "To All the Girls I've Loved Before," *Pancho & Lefty*, a duet album with Merle Haggard, "Seven Spanish Angels," one of my personal favorites, with Ray Charles. Willie even did a duet with then First Lady Rosalynn Carter of "Up Against the Wall Redneck Mother." Of course, the Highwaymen albums were the ultimate superstars' collaboration.

Over his lifetime, he has been active in charity projects. Perhaps most notable is his Farm Aid program. Willie helped start these concerts in 1985 to raise awareness about the loss of family farms and to raise funds to keep farm families on their land. It is are still an annual project where Willie is still performing as of 2023.

One of his 2017 projects that isn't history but related to the birth of country music is his collaboration in *The American Epic Sessions,* a documentary where an engineer restores the first electrical sound recording system from 1925 that Ralph Peer would have used in the Bristol Sessions. The film, directed and co-written by Bernard MacMahon, records songs from twenty contemporary artists in including a duet by Willie Nelson and Merle Haggard, "The Only Man Wilder Than Me," on the re-created machine that took over a decade to build from parts found all over the world. No original is still in existence.

The Willie Nelson and Friends Museum in Nashville began in 1979 when Willie opened it as the Willie Nelson and Family General Store. The museum tells not only about his life but lots about his friends. There's a Patsy Cline exhibit here with some of her belongings. Since he wrote Faron Young's big hit, "Hello Walls," there is a Faron Young exhibit too. Since Willie sang with almost every singer of every genre, there are many other stars represented here. You'll see lots of Willie's personal possessions, like his handmade domino table, his own billiard table, and more.

Willie has two sons to carry on his legacy, Mica and Lucas. Hopefully, as the last Highwaymen album says, *The Road Goes on Forever*.

Only a handful of musicians have left as large a footprint on country music as **Johnny Cash**. No question that he was an outlaw before the term related to music. His heartfelt performances in San Quentin and Folsom prisons led many people to believe Cash spent time in prison. Not so. He was arrested seven times on misdemeanor charges, usually related to his addictions.

The one that drove him to write a song about it happened on May 11, 1965, in Starkville, Mississippi, following a performance at the Mississippi State University and an unscheduled performance later at a fraternity house. Someone, probably a student, gave him a ride back to his motel where his future wife, June Carter, who also performed at the show, was in a separate room. Unable to sleep, a restless Cash when out in search of a place to buy a pack of cigarettes. Add together that this is one of the worst times of his addiction, a college campus, and a fraternity house, and you can imagine the shape Cash was in.

In the song, he says he was just picking flowers; dandelions and daises. The arrest warrant charged him with "public drunkenness, indecent exposure, and trespassing onto private property."

We all know when we have had a bit too much to drink and are walking around at night where there are no public restrooms what we will do about it. What better place to go than where a lot of dandelions and daises are growing wild?

In the song, he mentions that they threw him in jail and never even asked his name. That was why he was so mad that he kicked the cell walls so hard he broke his toe. A cellmate, a 15-year-old named Smokey Evans also booked for intoxication, benefited by the display of anger. Cash took off his shoes and gave them to Evans, saying, "Here's a souvenir. I'm Johnny Cash."

The next morning they let him out and fined him $36. By then, Cash's anger had passed. He invited the policeman who arrested him to attend one of his shows.

In 2007, Starkville pardoned Cash and refunded his $36 to his daughter, Kathy Cash. They held The Johnny Cash Flower Pickin' Festival to commemorate the jailing. Rosanne Cash sang and Marshall Grant, then the last surviving member of the Tennessee Three, played. Marty Stuart, Cash's lifelong friend and onetime son-in-law, sang "Starkville City Jail" playing a Gibson guitar similar to the one Cash used when he first played the song at Folsom Prison.

Fortunately, Cash got one other thing wrong in "Starkville City Jail." It was actually the Oktibbeha County Jail. At the festival, then-Oktibbeha-County-Sheriff Dolph Bryan commented he was glad of the mistake as Oktibbeha County Jail would not have sounded good. Today, there is a Mississippi Country Music Marker commemorating the jailing.

Over a lifetime of music, Cash hit the charts in pop, religious, blues, western, rockabilly, and rock, as well as country. His hits ranged across six decades and included a fan base from teens to seniors.

The Johnny Cash Museum in Nashville is rated number one music museum in the world and a must-see by *Forbes, Conde' Nast,* and *National Geographical Traveler.* There is a good reason. This museum covers his life from a kid in small town Dyess, Arkansas, to his death in 2003. More than just his music it portrays the real man. He had his flaws, but he never tried to pretend he was a saint; the museum does the same. By doing it they bring you a complete picture of the real Johnny Cash.

Cash's early life story is told with family photos from the 1940s in Dyess, Ark. That early home is also open as Historic Dyess Colony: Johnny Cash Boyhood Home, an Arkansas State University Heritage Site. It shows the history and culture of North East Arkansas where young Johnny Cash grew up. It is a great place to visit to understand how those early years influenced the singer's life later.

Then, every family had a radio like the one in the museum that young J. R. Cash, as he was called then, used to listen to the Grand Ole Opry. His Future Farmers of America member card and his school yearbook page remind you of his humble beginnings.

There is his old Martin guitar with a folded dollar bill stuck through the strings. Beneath is a note labeling it "My first professional guitar, 1955-'56." In those early days, he didn't have a drummer for the band, The Tennessee Two, so he used a dollar bill to give an illusion of a percussive instrument when he played the guitar. His early days at Sun Records are preserved here. One prized artifact is his platinum award for "Ring of Fire."

His stint in the air force is detailed here. His uniform is preserved in a glass case. Another exhibit shows Johnny Cash receiving the National Medal of Arts from President George Bush in a ceremony at Constitution Hall in 2002. Should anyone doubt his love for his country, they just need to read the words to the song he wrote, "The Ragged Old Flag," which tells the history of the American Flag.

There are tin cups and photos from Folsom Prison, where he recorded his iconic *Johnny Cash at Folsom Prison* album. His many awards and gold records are on display. When he began singing, vinyl records were the norm. His musical career ranged from those records on through 8-tracks, tapes, and CD. There are clips of Johnny Cash acting in films and TV dramas ranging from *Gospel Road: A Story of Jesus*, that he produced and financed himself in the early 70s, to roles he played such as *Five Minutes to Live* which stars Johnny Cash and Cay Forrester. Interestingly, for a very low-budget movie, the cast included two other well-known names, Ron Howard and singer, Merle Travis.

Johnny Cash, the author, is also represented there with Cash's three books. Papers, in his own handwriting and other documents, tell some of the motives and details behind *Man in Black, Man in White* and *Cash: The Autobiography*. It's also a little known fact that he also wrote poetry. A handwritten poem he wrote after June's funeral is displayed. There is a place in the museum that shows items related to the Carter family and his own family; most notably his brother, Tommy Cash, whose best-known record is "Six White Horses."

Looking at his life, you understand that Johnny Cash was so much more than a musician. He was a patriot, a rebel, a humanitarian, and most of all, he stands up for the downtrodden, as he says in his song, "The Man in Black."

His music related to that is best symbolized by his record, "The Ballad of Ira Hayes," about a Native American who enlisted in the marines and was one of the men who raised the flag at Iwo Jima. The song tells how Hayes was later denigrated and, at his death, "two inches of water in a lonely ditch was his grave." When disk jockeys refused to play the song, Cash called them out with a full-page ad in Billboard Magazine.

The last exhibit, and for me, the most moving one, is the video of him singing "Hurt." "Hurt" was recorded just seven months before his death and just a few months before June Carter Cash's death. It is so unbelievably sad that no words can do it justice. Thanks to modern technology, you can get your picture taken with Johnny Cash. I framed mine and will always treasure it.

You don't think of a Rhodes Scholar, an Oxford University graduate, and an army officer as an outlaw. **Kris Kristofferson** is all of those things and more. Kristofferson left the army in 1965 and moved to Nashville. He would work a week in Nashville as a part-time janitor at Columbia Records and a week in Lafayette, Louisiana, as a helicopter pilot for an oil company. While waiting on an oil platform and flying helicopters he wrote "Help Me Make It Through the Night," "Bobby McGee," and other songs destined to become hits. Then while working in Nashville, he'd try to pitch the songs. At Columbia Records, he met June Carter and gave her a demo tape of some of his songs and asked her to give it to Johnny Cash. She did, but it ended up in a big pile he already had from various songwriters. Kristofferson next did the famous helicopter landing on Johnny Cash's lawn. That got Cash to look at the songs. He loved "Sunday Morning Coming Down" and agreed to record it.

Cash's acceptance opened Music City doors for Kristofferson. He got a recording contract and recorded an album, *Kristofferson,* which didn't do great. He re-released it as *Me and Bobby McGee,* and it did better. His biggest success going into the 1970s was his songwriting. Other top singers recorded Kristofferson's songs including Waylon Jennings ("The Taker"), Gladys Knight & The Pips ("Help Me Make It Through The Night"), Bobby Bare ("Come Sundown"), Ray Price ("For the Good Times"), and many others. His "For the Good Times" sung by Ray Price won Song of the Year from the Academy of Country Music, and "Sunday Morning Coming Down" sung by Johnny Cash won the same award from the Country Music Association in 1970. Janis Joplin's recording of his "Me and Bobby McGee" released posthumously in 1971 on her album, *Pearl*, stayed at number 1 on both US and Australian charts for weeks and was certified platinum.

Kristofferson also achieved success in acting. He played in numerous movies and TV series. He won a Golden Globe Award as Best Actor for his role in *A Star Is Born*, with Barbara Streisand.

His participation in The Highwaymen brought a resurgence of many of his earlier less successful recordings to the forefront again. Kris Kristofferson's last full performance was on February 5, 2020 at the historic Sunrise Theater in Fort Pierce, Florida.

Merle Haggard was an outlaw legally. As a juvenile, he was in detention centers for everything from truancy to bad check writing. By the age of 20, he was serving time in San Quentin for attempted robbery. He was planning an escape with a fellow inmate but was sent to solitary for being caught drinking. While he was in solitary, the other inmate escaped, shot a policeman, was recaptured, and sentenced to death. Haggard straightened up. San Quentin released him on parole in 1960. One of those truth-is-stranger-than-fiction events that may have contributed to Haggard's decision to go straight and pursuing a music career is when Haggard watched Cash perform at San Quentin.

He stayed straight legally, and pursued his music career. In 1965, he had his first national top-10 record, "My Friends Are Gonna Be Strangers." It was about an unfaithful lover and not trusting anyone the future. Since

Haggard's ex-wife had a child by someone else while he was in prison, it must have resonated with him. His songs mostly related to prisoners. He released two albums in 1967 *I'm a Lonesome Fugitive* and *Branded Man*, where he sings about how, having once been in jail, a man could never hold his head up in pride. The title song from his album, *Sing me Back Home again*, is in memory of his friend, Jimmy "Rabbit" Kendrick in San Quentin, with whom he had planned to escape. The song is about a condemned man asking a friend with a guitar to play him a song as he goes to his execution. His next two albums, *The Legend of Bonnie and Clyde* and *Mamma Tried,* ranked number six and four respectively on Billboard's Country Chart. The title song "Mama Tried," about a young man who turned 21 while serving life in prison in spite of his mother's teachings. While he was doing a duet album with Willie in 1983, they felt it needed one blockbuster song, and thanks to Willie's daughter, Lana Nelson, they discovered "Pancho and Lefty" by songwriter Townes Van Zandt. They recorded it and named the album for it.

Willie Nelson Museum in Nashville

*(Top) Johnny Cash albums exhibit at Johnny Cash Museum in Nashville
(Bottom) Willie and band at St. Augustine Amphitheater*

Chapter 15 Gospel

Gospel music was a big influence on many musicians of the late 1940s and early '50s. Many of them began singing in churches where preachers and congregations yelled, stomped, and gyrated to choir music. To fully understand gospel music, we have to look back to England in the 1700s to a song still popular today, "Amazing Grace."

The song's composer, John Newton was an avid abolitionist and lived to see slavery peacefully banned in England. As a young man, he was active in the slave trade. On his first trip on a slave ship, he was abandoned in West Africa and enslaved in what is now Sierra Leone, he did learn some sympathy for enslaved people but when rescued he returned to the slave trade. He became an Anglican priest and in 1764, wrote "I cannot consider myself to have been a believer in the full sense of the word, until a considerable time afterwards."

As rector of St Mary Woolnoth Church, in London, he worked with the Committee for the Abolition of the Slave Trade. He became friends with the English poet, William Cowper. Cowper wrote the poem "The Negro's Complaint" that Martin Luther King Jr. often quoted. Cowper also wrote hymns. Together, they published "Amazing Grace" and other hymns for Shape Note Singing, in the hymnal, *Sacred Harp*. Evangelical preachers used Shape Note Singing because illiterate people easily understood it. It became popular in the American South in the early 19th century. Settlers carried the tradition into the Appalachians and the Ozarks. Church was where most singers of the early mountain music learned to sing. The Carter Family recorded gospel songs like "Up In My Father's House," "Sea Of Galilee," and "May The Circle be Unbroken." It all circled back and became a part of American music.

Like the poor mountain settlers, enslaved people were not literate. They were forced to adopt the religion of the enslavers. They often took those songs and used them as code to communicate among themselves about escaping or to pass information. "Go down, Moses" was Harriet

Tubman's calling card to identify herself to slaves who might want her to help them escape. Songs like "Steal Away" and "Wade In The Water" had double meaning. When a slave sang "Steal Away," it was code to other enslaved persons that they were going to seek to escape. "He calls me by the thunder" lets potential runaways know that stealing away during a storm was safer because the rains washed away scent that might allow the trackers and their dogs to find the escapee. "Wade In The Water" likewise warned runaways to "wade in water" to hide their scent from trackers. The words "God's a-going to trouble the water" tells them it may not be easy, but they needed to persevere.

The first recorded Black gospel song was "Swing Low, Sweet Chariot" by the **Fisk Jubilee Singers** in 1872.

There are some who call **Sister Rosetta Tharpe** "The Godmother of Rock and Roll." She was predominately a gospel singer, but her blend of screaming electric guitar, Delta blues, and New Orleans jazz, mixed with gospel, certainly helps that argument. Tharpe's 1945 recording, "Strange Things Happening Every Day" was the first gospel song to cross over to the "race music" charts, that were later renamed the R&B charts. The song reached No. two and was a huge influence on later rock 'n' roll. When asked about her influence on rock and roll, she stated, "Oh, these kids and rock and roll! This is just sped up rhythm and blues. I've been doing that forever."

Thomas A. Dorsey was born in Villa Rica, Georgia on July 1, 1899. He is often called "The Father of Gospel Music." His family moved to Atlanta when he was eight where he learned to play the piano at a nearby theater. By age 12, he was a professional musician, playing in the barrelhouses and brothels on Decatur Street in Atlanta. Dorsey played blues and came to be known as "Barrelhouse Tommy." He moved to Chicago at 17, where he attended music classes and worked day jobs and played the piano and sang blues in prohibition era speakeasies at night. He began composing songs for blues and jazz musicians in the early 1920s. He worked and performed with musicians, including Ma Rainey and Louis Armstrong. It was in Chicago that he had a "conversion" and wrote his very first gospel song, although he still performed blues and jazz.

In 1928, he wrote the song "Precious Lord, Take My Hand", one of the most popular gospel songs of all time. In the early 1930s, he focused exclusively on gospel music. He founded the National Convention of Gospel Choirs and Choruses and the Dorsey Music Company, which published gospel sheet music and recordings. Throughout his lifetime, he wrote many gospel songs, including "Take My Hand, Precious Lord" and "Peace in the Valley." Red Foley's cover of "Peace in the Valley," reached number seven on the Country & Western Best Seller chart and was among the first gospel recordings to sell a million copies. Dorsey's music combined elements of blues, jazz, and spirituals in his gospel songs. His songs were an inspiration for other gospel singers, including Mahalia Jackson.

Mahalia Jackson was born in the Black Pearl section of New Orleans, above Audubon Park near St. Charles Avenue. It was a convenient neighborhood of shotgun houses for people who worked for well-to-do St. Charles Avenue residents. She was raised strict Baptist and joined the church choir. Of course, no blues were allowed and dancing was only in church if the spirit moved you. However, her aunt's home where she grew up was next to a Pentecostal church and young Mahalia liked to listen to their more exuberant singing with clapping and foot stomping. She was surrounded by music, usually the blues being played in neighbors' houses. Second Line funeral processions, when the musicians played lively jazz, fascinated her. Her aunt's son, Fred, collected jazz and blues records and played them while his mother was at work. Mahalia grew to love the records by Bessie Smith, Mamie Smith, and Ma Rainey and would sing along while she worked around the house.

She moved to Chicago in the 1920s but the church her aunts attended there did not welcome her exuberant style of singing, although they allowed her to join the church choir. She joined a vocal group formed by the pastor's sons, Prince, Wilbur, and Robert Johnson, and Louise Lemon. The Johnson Singers was Chicago's first black gospel group.

She married Isaac "Ike" Hockenhull, but the marriage ended in an amicable divorce due to his gambling habit. The Johnson Singers disbanded in 1938, but Mahalia had saved enough money to get her beautician's license. She bought a building and opened a salon, across from Pilgrim Baptist Church, where Thomas Dorsey was the music director. Dorsey suggested they perform together to promote his music and her voice. They toured off and on until 1951. As she became more popular, her tours took her further from Chicago. In 1946, when she appeared at the Golden Gate Ballroom in Harlem, Art Freeman, a music scout for Apollo Records, heard her. Apollo had mostly jazz and blues artists and was looking to expand. They signed Jackson to a four-record session, letting her choose the songs. Her first two releases on Apollo did not sell well. About to drop her, they did one more session where she recorded "Move On Up a Little Higher." It was released in 1947.

Chicago radio personality, Louis "Studs" Terkel, heard it and played it on his show to his mostly white listeners. It was so well-received he interviewed her and had her sing it live. The song took the number two spot on the Billboard charts for two weeks, previously unheard of for gospel music. Apollo gave her another recording session, where she sang "Even Me" which sold one million and "Dig a Little Deeper" with almost a million sold. This put her popularity way over the top. She was invited to perform at a gospel music revue at Carnegie Hall. It was so popular it became a yearly event with Mahalia headlining.

She left Apollo when she found they were withholding her royalties and became the first gospel artist to sign with Columbia. Touring extensively both in the States and abroad, she had difficulty finding lodging while touring in the South due to Jim Crow laws. During the '60s, she became active in the Civil Right Movement and was close friends with Doctor Martin Luther King, Jr. and Ralph Abernathy. She marched with Dr. King in the March on Washington for Jobs and Freedom and sang "I've Been 'Buked and I've Been Scorned" on King's request, then "How I Got Over." She sang at the Democratic National Convention in 1956 and campaigned for Kennedy and sang at his inaugural ball in 1961. Mahalia appeared with Johnny Cash and Flip Wilson on television shows and played in several movies.

She was invited to a symposium on how to define jazz. The audience was mostly writers and students of jazz and Mahalia's singing was often considered jazz or blues with religious lyrics. One participant asked how much gospel music come from jazz? She replied, "Baby, don't you know the Devil stole the beat from the Lord?"

Business-wise, she prospered. One of her ventures was with Grand Ole Opry star, Minnie Pearl, in a chain of restaurants called Mahalia Jackson's Chicken Dinners.

In spite of her busy schedule, she was lonely and married again. Sigmond Galloway proved abusive both physically and mentally, and the marriage ended in divorce. Mahalia Jackson died in 1972 and is buried near her birthplace in Metairie, Louisiana.

I heard **Mavis Staples** sing "Wade in the Water" in St. Augustine in 2015 and will never forget the passion she gave that song. Besides being a prolific gospel singer, she performed rhythm and blues and was a civil rights activist. She was born in Chicago in 1939 and learned to sing in church. Her career began as a member of her family's band The Staple Singers, once called "God's greatest hitmakers."

She has won many honors. She is the recipient of the Grammy Lifetime Achievement Award, three Grammy Awards, including Album of the Year. Staples was inducted into the Rock and Roll Hall of Fame in 1999, and in the Gospel Music Hall of Fame as a member of The Staple Singers in 2018, named a Kennedy Center Honoree in 2016, inducted into the Blues Hall of Fame as a soloist in 2017, and received the inaugural Rock Hall Honors Award from the Rock and Roll Hall of Fame, as a soloist in 2019. Rolling Stone named her one of the "100 Greatest Singers of all Time" in 2008. She was nominated for a 2004 Grammy Award with Bob Dylan in the "Best Pop Collaboration With Vocals" category for their duet on "Gonna Change My Way of Thinking", from the album *Gotta Serve Somebody: The Gospel Songs of Bob Dylan*. Dylan proposed to her, but she turned him down. She was married briefly to Spencer Leak in 1964, but he wanted her to give up her career and stay at home.

The Staple Singers signed with Stax Records in 1968, and hit the Top 40 eight times between 1971 and 1975. They had two No. 1 singles, "I'll Take You There" and "Let's Do It Again." In 1996 she did the album *Spirituals & Gospels: A Tribute to Mahalia Jackson* to honor Mahalia Jackson, who was a significant influence and close family friend. Another, *That's What I Say*, was dedicated to Ray Charles. She appeared in TV shows and movies and performed the title song in 1989's National Lampoon's Christmas Vacation. *Mavis!*, a documentary about Mavis and the Staple Singers, premiered at the South by Southwest Film Festival in March 2015 and was broadcast on HBO in February 2016. It won a Peabody Award.

(Top) Mavis Staples at St. Augustine 450 birthday event (Bottom) Rosetta Tharp exhibit at Cleveland Rock and Roll Hall of Fame

Chapter 16 R&B and Soul

Soul music grew out of rhythm and blues. Rhythm and blues, often referred to as R&B, and soul music are both genres of African-American music or early blues. As you learned in the blues chapter, blues had an origin in gospel and music brought from the singers' homeland. Most of the R&B and Soul singers began singing in gospel groups in their churches.

In the 1960s, as Civil Rights activism demanded all people be treated equally, soul arose. It had a more gospel-inspired vocal style with the passion and intensity of some emotional preachers and often dealt with feeling like love and loss. R&B may be a smoother vocal on any theme. R&B may have more electronic instruments, like synthesizers and drum machines. While there are these differences between the two genres, many of the songs fit in both. Since they are closely intertwined and many of the same musicians contributed to both, I am lumping them together here. These musicians were talented individuals, so many of their songs also fit other genera like rock and roll. Music journalist turned record producer, Jerry Wexler, first coined the term R&B in 1948 to replace "race music" as it had been called.

According to **Otis Redding**'s biography, soul music is "music that arose out of the black experience in America through the transmutation of gospel and rhythm and blues into a form of funky, secular testifying."

Otis Redding is known as The King of Soul. Although he was not the first soul singer, one of his songs usually scores the top spot on any list of the best soul songs; "RESPECT," which he wrote and first recorded in 1965. However, the recording usually hitting that top spot is Aretha Franklin's version.

Otis Redding blazed across the music skyline like a shooting star. Early in his career, he sang with Little Richard's band. He cited Little Richard as one of his main influences saying, "I entered the music business because of Richard—he is my inspiration. I used to sing like Little Richard, his rock 'n' roll stuff."

"(Sittin' on) The Dock of the Bay" is Redding's most famous song and one of the most popular soul songs of all time. His "Try a Little Tenderness," recorded for Stax Records, begins slow and soulful but builds into a frenetic R&B ending. It has elements from the Duke Ellington–Lee Gaines song "Just Squeeze Me (But Please Don't Tease Me,)" a jazz number.

Like that shooting star, Redding's life burned out way too soon. He died in a plane crash in 1967 at the age of 26.

The Stax Museum of American Soul Music is another Memphis place you need to visit to learn about soul music. The Otis Redding exhibit at Stax has many artifacts from Redding's life, plus lots more about soul music. I loved the reconstruction of a simple country church recognizing the influence gospel had on soul music. Move from simple to over-the-top with Stax Records musician Isaac Hayes' gold-plated Cadillac.

In 1960, Jim Stewart and his sister Estelle Axton, opened Stax in a former theater. Today, the museum is housed in a perfect reconstruction of the original building. Some of the '60s greatest music came out of Stax.

Stax ignored the color barrier. White and Black musicians worked together with mutual respect. **Booker T. & the M.G.'s,** the house band at Stax Records, was a mixed group. Booker T. Jones on organ and piano, Al Jackson Jr. on drums, and Lewie Steinberg on bass, were Black; Steve Cropper on guitar was white, Steinberg was later replaced by Donald "Duck" Dunn, who was white. They were considered one of the first racially integrated bands in a music form considered part of Black culture. The group had their own hit, "Green Onions," that went to the top of the R&B Chart and number 3 on the Pop Chart. They backed Rufus and Carla Thomas, Aretha Franklin, Otis Redding, Wilson Pickett, and many others.

Just like rock and roll, it's hard to pinpoint the birth of R&B. One musician often cited as first R&B musician is bandleader and saxophonist **Louis Jordan**, a swing jazz musician who co-composed the 1944 hit song "Is You Is or Is You Ain't My Baby." He used the shuffle rhythm, boogie-woogie bass lines, and short horn riffs with vocal call-and-response.

Another early R&B originator is Cab Calloway. I still would classify both of them as jazz musicians and both songs predate the first use of the term R&B.

Pioneering R&B groups in the late 1940s and early 50s are not well known today. Even then, their music made little impact. Groups like the Dunbar Four/Hi Fi's, The Cardinals, the Four Bars of Rhythm, the Five Blue Notes, the Melodaires, the Armstrong Four, and the Clovers. The musicians of these bands were mostly born before 1935 and came of age about 1947. They reflected the post-war movement of many African Americans to the bigger cities.

Ray Charles has been called "the genius of soul." One of the pioneers of soul music, he was born in Albany, Georgia in 1930. Blind since the age of 7, he defied the odds to become one of the foremost icons in the history of American music. His first R&B song "Baby Let Me Hold Your Hand" released in 1951, jumped to #5 on the nation's R&B chart. He grew up in the small town of Greenville, near Tallahassee, Florida and attended St. Augustine's School for the Deaf and Blind where he learned to play piano, organ, clarinet, trumpet, and saxophone.

During the 1950s, he had several career milestones. He signed with Atlantic Records and scored his first No. 1 hit with "I Got a Woman." That song combined elements of gospel music with blues and was one of the first of the new musical genre, soul music. In 1959, he once more topped the R&B chart with "What'd I Say." It was Charles' first crossover hit. He had hits in so many genres it's hard to keep track. The hit songs included "Hit the Road Jack," "You Don't Know Me," "Crying Time," and "Georgia on My Mind," which became his signature song. Most were also pop music hits. He scored his first #1 county hit in a duo with Willie Nelson, "Seven Spanish Angels." His "We Didn't See a Thing" with George Jones and Chet Atkins, placed in the top 10 on the country chart.

A film depicting Charles' life, *Ray,* was released in 2004 shortly after Charles' death. Jamie Foxx, won the 2004 Academy Award for Best Actor for his portrayal of Ray Charles.

Clyde McPhatter, singing with **The Drifters**, hit number 1 on the chart in 1953 with "Money Honey." He began his singing career in gospel music like so many other R&B singers. His professional career began in 1950, singing with Billy Ward and His Dominoes. His powerful tenor voice and emotional delivery earned the Dominoes a string of hits, including "Have Mercy Baby," "Do Something for Me," and "Sixty Minute Man."

He was drafted into the army in 1954 and began a solo career after he was released. His biggest hits as a solo artist were "A Lover's Question" and "Lover Please." He died of a heart attack in 1972 at the age of 39.

Hank Ballard and the Midnighters' "Work with Me, Annie" was an R&B hit in 1954, spending seven weeks at number 1 on the R&B charts along with the answer songs "Annie Had a Baby" and "Annie's Aunt Fannie." He was the original writer/singer of the huge **Chubby Checker** hit song, "The Twist." He was a singer and songwriter whose work crossed over from R&B to rock and roll.

The Civil Rights movement of the 1960s brought R&B artists and songwriters to the public eye. R&B music of that time began to focus on the social issues. One that caught a lot of attention was **Sam Cooke**'s "A Change Is Gonna Come." Cooke was born in 1931 in Clarksdale, Mississippi, famous for its blues. So, no surprise, his music blending in his early gospel training helped make soul music a mainstream item. In the late 1950s and early 1960s, he had a string of hits including "You Send Me," "Chain Gang," and "Twistin' the Night Away." He was one of the first R&B singers to address issues of poverty, racism, and war in his music. He was murdered in Los Angeles in 1963 at the age of 33.

James Brown was known as the "Godfather of Soul." "Say It Loud—I'm Black and I'm Proud" and "I Don't Want Nobody to Give Me Nothing (Open Up the Door, I'll Get It Myself)," were anthems of the Civil Rights movement. He had a string of other hits including "Papa's Got a Brand New Bag," "I Got You (I Feel Good)," and "It's a Man's Man's Man's World." His music crossed over to the pop field as well. James Brown grew up in Augusta, Georgia and the city honors him with a statue downtown. The Augusta Museum of History has an extensive exhibit on him.

Marvin Gaye's *What's Going On* Album was a big hit as well as raising consciousness about inequities in society. Gaye's soul music was characterized by its strong vocals, gospel roots, and social commentary. He was another of the earliest soul singers to address issues of poverty, racism, and war in his music.

Gaye's vocals had a four-octave vocal range, and he could convey a wide range of emotions through his songs. He wrote songs about his own experiences, and he often used his music to explore themes of love, loss, and redemption in them, using his voice to create a sense of drama and urgency. His songs "What's Going On" and "Mercy Mercy Me (The Ecology)" are two examples of his social commentary in soul music.

Wilson Pickett began his career singing in Baptist church choirs in his hometown of Prattville, Alabama. In 1955, he moved to Detroit, Michigan, where he joined another gospel group, The Violinaires. They had no major successes. In 1959, Pickett joined the Falcons, a rhythm and blues group. They had a few hits, including "You're So Fine" and "I Found a Love." In 1963, Pickett left to go solo.

Pickett's solo career was most successful with "In the Midnight Hour." that reached #1 on the Billboard R&B chart and #2 on the Billboard Hot 100 chart. Pickett recorded for a variety of labels throughout his career, including Stax and Atlantic. In early 1966, Jerry Wexler from Atlantic Records took Pickett to FAME Studios in Muscle Shoals, where he backed by the Muscle Shoals "Swampers" recorded some of his biggest hits such as "Land of A Thousand Dances" and "Mustang Sally." In 1987, he moved on to record at Motown where he released the album *Pickett's Got Next*. The album included the singles "Fire and Water" and "I'm a Midnight Mover." It was only a moderate success reaching #43 on the Billboard 200 chart. He died in 2006 at the age of 64.

Unlike other fields, R&B and soul did not shut women out. **Aretha Franklin** earned the title "Queen of Soul" as one of the best-selling artists of all time. She began singing gospel in her father's church. He was the pastor of New Bethel Baptist Church in

Detroit, Michigan. Aretha began a professional career as a gospel singer, with her father managing her.

When she turned 18, she told him she wanted to be a pop singer, and he agreed. They moved to New York, and she signed with Columbia Records in 1960 and remained with them until 1965. She had some records that charted and built a fan base, but was not a commercial success.

In 1966, Producer Jerry Wexler convinced her to move to Atlantic Records. Wexler felt her gospel background lent itself well to the new form of R&B being identified as soul. In January 1967, she recorded "I Never Loved a Man (The Way I Love You)", backed by the Muscle Shoals Rhythm Section at FAME Studios in Muscle Shoals, Alabama. The trip was a mixed bag. Franklin only spent one day recording at FAME, because a fight broke out between her manager and husband, Ted White, studio owner, Rick Hall, and a horn player. However, when the song was released the following month, it raced to number one on the R&B chart, and number nine on the Billboard Hot 100, giving Franklin her first top-ten pop single. (More about FAME Studio and the Muscle Shoals sound later.)

Her cover of Otis Redding's "Respect" and her "(You Make Me Feel Like) A Natural Woman" became an anthem for the Civil Rights movement and for women's rights. She was also a strong supporter of Native American rights. She was the first woman inducted into the Rock and Roll Hall of Fame in 1987 and was awarded the Presidential Medal of Freedom in 2005 by then President George W. Bush.

Perhaps President Obama's statement about her when she performed at the White House in 2015 sums it up best.

> Nobody embodies more fully the connection between the African-American spiritual, the blues, R. & B., rock and roll—the way that hardship and sorrow were transformed into something full of beauty and vitality and hope. American history wells up when Aretha sings. That's why, when she sits down at a piano and sings "A Natural Woman," she can move me to tears—the same way that Ray Charles's version of "America the Beautiful" will always be in my view the most patriotic piece of music ever performed—because it captures the fullness of the American experience, the view from the bottom as well as the top, the good and the bad, and the possibility of synthesis, reconciliation, transcendence.

Aretha Franklin along with several other performers declined to take part in Donald Trump's 2017 inauguration as an act of musical protest.

Etta James bridged the gaps between genres ranging from jazz, R&B, soul, rock 'n roll, gospel and blues. She was honored with more than thirty awards ranging from the Rock and Roll Hall of Fame, the Rhythm and Blues Foundation, The Blues Hall of Fame, and the Rockabilly Hall of Fame. Born Jamesetta Hawkins on January 25, 1938 in Los Angeles, California to a 14-year-old mother, she never knew her father but believed he was a professional pool player named Minnesota Fats. She was raised in a series of foster homes and by relatives.

Jamesetta got her first musical break when she was 14, performing with an all-girls group of light-complexioned Black girls who called themselves The Creolettes. She met musician, talent scout, and record producer, Johnny Otis, who got them a contract with Modern Records. At his suggestion, the group changed their name to Peaches and young Jamesetta did a play on her first name and became Etta James.

In early 1961, she released "At Last," composed by Glenn Miller, which reached number two on the R&B chart and number 47 on the Billboard Hot 100. It's considered her signature song.

In the early '60s, she began adding a gospel touch to many of her songs like "Something's Got a Hold on Me" and "Stop the Wedding."

Over her many years performing, her name was linked with many famous performers. While still singing with Peaches, they were an opening act for Little Richard's national tour. She dated B.B. King when she was 16 and believed that King's "Sweet Sixteen" was about her. In early 1955, she and young Elvis Presley, who was then recording for Sun Studios, also a fan of King's, played jointly in a club near Memphis. She sang background when recording for Chess for Chuck Berry on his "Back in the USA." In 1978, she was the opening act for the Rolling Stones. Once again, she appeared with Chuck Berry in 1987 for a joint performance of "Rock and Roll Music" in the documentary film *Hail! Hail! Rock 'n' Roll*.

She added a bit of rock to her 1978 album *Deep in the Night*, produced by Jerry Wexler for Warner Bros., incorporated more rock-based music in her repertoire. She even added a touch of hip hop in later years when she collaborated with rap singer Def Jef on his song "Droppin' Rhymes on Drums."

Sadly, alcoholism and heroin addiction caused a halt to her recording from the late 70s to mid 80s. Etta James covered a lot of musical territory in her career. She died on January 20, 2012.

Irma Thomas was another member of soul royalty. Her powerful and emotive vocal style earned her the title "Soul Queen of New Orleans." I remember hearing her sing "It's Raining" at a local sock hop and loved her voice. She was born on February 18, 1941, in Ponchatoula, Louisiana.

Like many other R&B singers, she began singing in her Baptist church choir. Throughout her career, Irma Thomas had numerous hit songs and albums, with some of her most notable tracks including "Time Is on My Side," "Wish Someone Would Care," and "It's Raining." "Time Is on My Side" became one of her signature songs and was later covered by The Rolling Stones.

In 2007, she won her first Grammy for Best Contemporary Blues Album for *After the Rain*. In April 2007, she was inducted into the Louisiana Music Hall of Fame. She usually performs at the annual New Orleans Jazz & Heritage Festival.

New Orleans has its own version of R&B starting with **Professor Longhair** sometimes known as "Fess." Born Henry Roeland "Roy" Byrd on December 19, 1918, much like traditional Louisiana cooking, he somewhat bridges the gap between old time blues and R&B with a touch of jazz, Caribbean, and boogie woogie thrown in to make it unique. Part of the reason that his piano style is so different is that he learned to play on a piano with missing keys. Much of his influence is seen in the music of other New Orleans greats, such as Fats Domino, Allen Toussaint, and Dr. John.

If you visit New Orleans, especially at Mardi Gras, you will hear his favorites, "Tipitina" and "Go to the Mardi Gras." Another uniquely New Orleans song he recorded is "Big Chief" telling about the New Orleans Mardi Gras Indians that dress in elaborate handmade Indian costumes and march to their own beat for Mardi Gras.

It's not often a musician has a facility named for his song, but Professor Longhair does. Local music enthusiasts opened the venue on January 14, 1977 and named it for his song, "Tipitina." Professor

Longhair performed there until his death in 1980. There's a bronze bust of the Professor inside with his traditional sunglasses. Before it was named Tipitina's, it was called "The 501 Club," because of its address at 501 Napoleon Avenue. Tipitina's is one of New Orleans' best-known clubs today. The building was constructed in 1912, and had many incarnations during its lifetime, including a gambling house, gymnasium, and brothel.

Malcolm John Rebennack Jr. better known by his stage name **Dr. John** was born November 20, 1941. He has the typical melting pot of New Orleans cultures, German, Irish, Spanish, English, and French heritage. His music combined New Orleans blues, jazz, funk, and R&B. In 1955 When he was about 13 years old, Rebennack met Professor Longhair and for a time played in his band.

While he was still a student at Jesuit High School, he formed his first band, The Dominoes, and started playing in nightclubs. As anyone familiar with the Jesuit's ideas will know, the good fathers disapproved of that. They ordered him to stop playing in clubs or leave the school. Rebennack quit school in 1954 and focused entirely on his music.

By the late 1950s he was playing around the country with another of his bands, Mac Rebennack and the Skyliners. His career as a guitarist ended around 1960 when he was shot and the ring finger of his left hand was injured while playing in Jacksonville, Florida. From then on, he concentrated on bass guitar and later piano as his main instrument.

Shortly after that, he was arrested for using and selling narcotics and running a brothel. He was arrested and sentenced to two years in the Federal Correctional Institution in Fort Worth. When he was released in 1965 he headed west to Los Angeles where he became a session musician until the 1970s.

As a young man, he became interested in Voodoo, and while in Los Angeles, he came up with an idea of a Dr. John character based a voodoo priest he knew of in New Orleans, Dr. John, who came to New Orleans from Haiti and sold gris-gris, animal parts, and other items used in the voodoo religion. Originally, the idea was for Rebennack to produce the record and stage show on Dr. John as part of the culture of New Orleans with a friend reenacting "Dr. John", while Rebennack did the music and production. The friend backed out and Rebennack became "Dr. John" releasing his album, *Gris-Gris*, in January 1968.

His act combined New Orleans-style rhythm and blues with psychedelic rock and elaborate stage shows that bordered on voodoo religious ceremonies brought him some recognition as a solo artist.

In 1972, he recorded *Gumbo*, an album of traditional New Orleans music from the late 1940s and 1950s. "Iko Iko," hit Billboard Hot 100 singles chart, reaching No. 71. It's a song about the Mardi Gras Indians. "Iko Iko" was a victory chant and "Jock-A-Mo" was a chant the Indians did going into battle. In the Indians, there are ranks with chief being highest. Flag boy next highest and spy boy ranks close behind. My favorite part of the song is where one chief tells another his spy boy is gonna' set your flag on fire. Various other artists change this to other persona doing something different. Dr. John's *Gumbo* was ranked number 404 on Rolling Stone Magazine's list of the 500 greatest albums of all time.

Dr. John continued to record for the rest of his life with even a posthumous country & western album released September 23, 2022, *Things Happen That Way,* with guests Aaron Neville, Willie Nelson, and Lukas Nelson recorded the year he died, 2019. In November, 2022, it was nominated for a Grammy for Best Americana Album.

It's hard to categorize **Allen Toussaint**. Yes, he was a musician. He recorded his first album *The Wild Sound of New Orleans* as Al Tousan for RCA Records in 1958. Songs ranged from "Chokin' Kind" previously sung by Waylon Jennings as a country hit to "Cast Your fate to the Wind" a true jazz number. His most significant albums are *From a Whisper to a Scream* released in 1971 is considered a funk, jazz and soul album, and *Southern Nights* released in 1975 is considered a pivotal album in the development of New Orleans R&B.

He was a producer and, with Marshall Sehorn, creator of Sansu Enterprises and Sansu record label, with the Sea-Saint recording studio in the Gentilly section of New Orleans.

Some of his biggest accomplishments were his songwriting. He often wrote using his mother's maiden name, Naomi Neville, as a pseudonym Some of his most famous songs were Ernie K-Doe's "Mother'-in-Law" Irma Thomas' "It's Raining" and "Ruler of My Heart." The latter was adapted by Otis Redding, who claimed credit as writer, and recorded at Stax under the title "Pain in My Heart." Toussaint filed a lawsuit against Redding and Stax and the claim was settled out of court, with Stax agreeing to credit Naomi Neville as the songwriter.

Toussaint produced Aaron Neville's records on the Minit label in the early 1960s, including "Over You" and "Let's Live," and again in the 1970s on "Hercules" and "The Greatest Love." He worked with another Neville brother, Art Neville, later of the Neville Brothers group, when he played with instrumental funk group The Meters on several of his records including their hit "Cissy Strut." Incidentally, in spite of Toussaint's mother having the same last name, he's not related to the Neville Brothers.

Aaron Neville and **Neville Brothers** need a mention because they are part of the New Orleans musical tradition. As a group they first recorded together in 1976, when the four brothers, Art, Charles, Aaron, and Cyril took part in an album of the same name by *The Wild Tchoupitoulas*, led by their uncle, George Landry who was "Big Chief Jolly" in the tribe. Note this is a Mardi Gras Indian tribe, not a Native American tribe. The album is a collection of songs representing chants and fight songs of the group. Another New Orleans band, The Meters, where Art Neville was already doing vocals and playing the keyboard, provided part of the instrumentation. It was recorded at Allan Toussaint's Sea-Saint Studios. The album was added to the US Library of Congress' National Registry In 2012 for "cultural, artistic and historic importance to the nation's aural legacy."

The album encouraged the Neville brothers to cut an album of their own, *The Neville Brothers,* in 1978. All the brothers had musical experience prior to joining together. Art had gained prominence for his band's version of "Mardi Gras Mambo," which had become a classic shortly after they recorded it in 1954. Aaron and Cyril had played with The Meters and in its earlier incarnations. Charles had an interest in music, but his drug addiction landed him in Louisiana State Penitentiary at Angola in 1963, where he served three and a half years for possession of marijuana. He honed his saxophone talents practiced in the prison music room with other incarcerated New Orleans musicians and went to New York to begin playing with various bands there when he was released.

They released *Fiyo on the Bayou* in 1981, which included "Iko Iko" and continued performing until 2012. The group's most successful songs were "Yellow Moon," "Sister Rosa," and "Healing Chant," all released in the 1980s and 1990s.

Aaron's son Ivan joined the group in its later years. Aaron's first major hit single was "Tell It Like It Is." It sold over a million copies and won a gold record. The song topped Billboard's R&B chart for five weeks in 1967 and placed No. 2 on the Billboard Hot 100.

Aaron ventured into country music In 1993 with his album The Grand Tour. He followed that with a duet with Trisha Yearwood on 1994's Rhythm, *Country and Blues*, an album of duets each by R&B and Country artists including Little Richard and Tanya Tucker doing "Somethin' Else." Neville and Yearwood recorded "I Fall to Pieces," a former hit for Patsy Cline back in 1961. Neville and Yearwood won the Grammy Award for Best Country Collaboration with Vocals at the 37th Annual Grammy Awards, making Neville one of the few African American artists to win a Grammy in the country genre.

Aaron retired from touring in 2021 but may continue to perform at festivals and make records. Incidentally, the Neville family is of mixed African-American, white, and Choctaw heritage, so those Indian songs come naturally from blood and Mardi Gras Indian connections.

(Top) Rock and Soul Museum in Memphis
(Bottom) Isaac Hayes' gold-plated Cadillac at Stax

(Top) Rock and Soul Museum exhibit in Memphis (Bottom) Little Richard exhibit in Tubman Museum in Macon

Otis Redding statue in Macon

(Top) Ray Charles Memorial Albany, GA
(Bottom) James Brown exhibit at Augusta Museum of History, Augusta, GA

Chapter 17 Motown

The musical legacy of much of Detroit's music has its roots in the Great Migration of the early 20th Century. African Americans and equally poor folks from the mountains of Appalachia made their way to Detroit in search of jobs. They brought their musical roots with them and in the mid-twentieth century that melted into what became Rock and Roll.

In 1959, **Berry Gordy Jr.** began the music label that changed the world forever. The Empire on West Grand Blvd consisted of the eight buildings where Motown Records operated until 1968. The street has been renamed Berry Gordy Jr. Blvd. We started in the original business offices. After the business moved, Berry Gordy's sister, Esther Gordy Edwards, saw the need to create a museum to showcase the early days of Motown. *The Motown Sound*, a 15-minute video, takes you through the early history.

It starts when Berry Gordy received a royalty check for a song he wrote for $3.19. Smokey Robinson saw it and told him, "If that's what you are going to earn, you might as well be in business for yourself."

That's exactly what Gordy did. Using $800 borrowed from his family, he began Motown Records. Gordy is famous mostly for the groups he recorded, although he recorded some top-notch solo acts like Marvin Gay and Smokey Robinson. He said, "I want to make music with a great story and a great beat that everyone can enjoy,"

The world was changed because of that. **Smokey Robinson** sums up why Motown was important not only musically but as a civic milestone. "When we would go to the South and do shows. On one side of the stage would be white people and on the other side were Black people. Total separatism. And by the time we would be finishing up, not only would they be talking and laughing, they'd be dancing together. It was a great time for progress and people of good will were coming together and saying, 'Hey, there's a little bit of me in you and a little bit of you in me.'"

Smokey Robinson's contributions to the world of music, particularly in the realms of R&B, soul, and pop, have left an indelible mark. Born William "Smokey" Robinson on February 19, 1940, in Detroit, was one of the first artists Berry signed to Motown Records, and played a vital role in the label's rise to prominence in the 1960s. He served as a vice president of Motown and was deeply involved in the creative and business aspects of the company.

Besides working solo, Robinson co-founded the vocal group **The Miracles,** which including Warren "Pete" Moore and Ronald White, in the 1950s. They signed with Motown Records in 1957. Robinson wrote many of The Miracles' hit songs, including "Shop Around," "You've Really Got a Hold on Me," and "The Tracks of My Tears."

He won numerous awards and honors throughout his career, both as a member of The Miracles and as a solo artist, including multiple Grammy Awards, the Kennedy Center Honors, and induction into the Rock and Roll Hall of Fame.

While Smokey Robinson primarily worked with The Miracles, he also wrote a few songs for **The Supremes**, including "The Composer" and "When the Lovelight Starts Shining Through His Eyes." In 1967, Berry Gordy renamed the group Diana Ross & the Supremes. They achieved mainstream success with **Diana Ross** as lead singer. Their "Where Did Our Love Go" reached number one on the US pop charts and was their first song to appear on the UK singles chart, where it reached number three. Ross later went on to a successful career as a solo act.

The Marvelettes had one of the first number-one singles recorded by an all-female vocal group and the first by a Motown recording act with their 1961 "Please Mr. Postman." They later benefited from Robinson's songwriting with "Don't Mess with Bill" and "The Hunter Gets Captured by the Game."

The **Four Tops** helped define the Motown sound of the 1960s. They ranged from soul, R&B, disco, adult contemporary, doo wop, jazz, and show tunes. They remained together for over four decades, from 1953 until 1997, without a change in members. You'll see suits worn by the Four Tops in the museum section of Motown.

They had their first number one hit, "I Can't Help Myself (Sugar Pie, Honey Bunch)" in June 1965, followed by many others including

"It's the Same Old Song" (1965), "Something About You" (1965), "Shake Me, Wake Me (When It's Over)" (1966), "Loving You Is Sweeter Than Ever" (1966) and "Still Water (Love) (1970)."

Showing the relationship between music genres, The Four Tops recorded "If I Were a Carpenter" in 1967, and it scored on 17 on R&B chart and 20 on pop. In 1970, Johnny Cash and June Carter recorded it as well. Their version went to No. 2 on the country chart and No. 36 on pop.

The Four Tops sang backup on The Supremes songs ("Run, Run, Run," 1964), **Martha and the Vandellas** ("My Baby Loves Me," 1966 hit) and others. The group recorded under different names with other labels, but it was after signing with Motown in 1962, the Vandellas had a charting hit with their second release, "Come and Get These Memories." It reached number twenty-nine on the Billboard Hot 100 and peaking at number six on the R&B chart. Their second hit, "Heat Wave", reaching number four on the Hot 100 and held number one on the R&B singles chart for five weeks. It was their first million-seller and earned the group their only Grammy Award nomination for Best R&B Performance. In 1970, the Vandellas recorded Motown's first protest single, the controversial anti-war song, "I Should Be Proud." It peaked at forty-five on the R&B singles chart.

Gordy changed the name to Martha Reeves and the Vandellas in 1967. The group disbanded in 1972 due to members infighting.

Although groups were big at Motown, there were some outstanding solo acts. Marvin Gaye, who I wrote about in the Rhythm and Blues Chapter, and **Mary Wells.** Smokey Robinson wrote and produced many of Mary Wells' early hits, including "My Guy," which became one of her signature songs and a Motown classic.

There is a hat and silver glove at the museum from one of the biggest names to record at Motown. **Michael Jackson** recorded here as a child with his siblings as **The Jackson Five**. The Jackson Five consisted of brothers Jackie, Tito, Jermaine, Marlon, and Michael. Managed by their father Joe Jackson, they were one of the first African American groups to attain a crossover following. They began performing in 1964, when Michael was five years old. Jackie, the oldest of the brothers, was 12. March 1968 was their first paying gig when they opened for Etta James at the Apollo Theater.

The Jackson Five signed an exclusive seven-year contract with Motown on March 11, 1969. They released "I Want You Back" in 1969 and topped the Billboard Hot 100 chart for seven weeks. It was also a number one hit in the United Kingdom, Canada, and Australia. They rapidly became a worldwide phenomenon. Fans would mob them at airports and on the street. They now required bodyguards wherever they went. A normal childhood was no longer possible for the brothers. As the youngest, Michael would have been the most impacted.

Throughout the '70s, they had a string of number one hits, "ABC" (1970), "The Love You Save" (1970), "I'll Be There" (1970), "Never Can Say Goodbye" (1971), "Maybe Tomorrow" (1971), "Lookin' Through the Windows" (1972), "Dancing Machine" (1974), "All I Do Is Think of You" (1975), and others. They ended their contract with Motown in March 1976. Since Motown owned the name "Jackson Five," they called themselves The Jacksons.

By now Michael was released solo songs and albums. His *Off the Wall* album success literally was off the wall. About this time, Michael split from the group and released his second Epic album, in November 1982, as *Thriller*, which became the best-selling album of all time, winning eight Grammy Awards, including Album of the Year. It included two number-one hit singles, "Billie Jean" and "Beat It", and three breakthrough MTV music videos, "Billie Jean", "Beat It", and the zombie-themed music video "Thriller." This moved him out of the historic period and into modern times as "The King of Pop."

Motown was part of the music of my mid-teen years when the country was under tremendous stress. The Vietnam War was killing off young men by the thousands. Civil Rights were being recognized slowly. We were approaching the Nixon era of the most dishonest political climate the country had seen up to that time. Yet the happy bouncy songs of Motown's artist made everyone want to dance and sing along.

The exhibits at Motown museum showcase those singers and songs. One wall is showcases album covers. I still have a few of those albums.

Another fun thing to do here is sing in the studio. Mike McLean, a young engineer with Motown, created a precursor to the present day synthesizer echo chamber. He created it by cutting a hole in the ceiling putting in speakers, so you come out with a bigger vocal sound.

The museum tells how Berry Gordy formed Motown. He worked an assembly line at Ford Motor Company, a job he hated, but as our guide told us, it was a "Blessing in disguise because he began writing lyrics in his head in time to the rhythms of the assemble line."

Another thing Gordy took from assembly line work was the rough crude metal that began at the beginning of the line and became a shining star when it emerged. He wanted to do the same with his musicians. He hired Maxine Powell to turn his rough-cut diamonds into sparkling gems. She not only taught the singers stage presence, but grooming, poise, and social graces. She made Motown's artists looked sharp and move smoothly and naturally when they performed.

Part of what you will see when you visit Hitsville is the first home Berry Gordon bought. He and his family lived on the second floor, and the first floor was Hitsville, USA and Studio A. The Gordy apartment was simple. The family's dining room table was often used as a shipping desk in the early days.

You reach the climax of the tour standing in Studio A singing and dancing to "My Girl." **The Temptations** were another group Smokey Robinson helped by writing "My Girl" and other hit songs for. Other hits they had included "Get Ready." and "The Way You Do the Things You Do."

It's a thrill to be in the same studio where these stars recorded. It's only the only place on the tour you are allowed to take inside pictures. The control room, separated from the main studio by a glass, was originally a small kitchen. The studio was a garage remodeled by Mr. Gordy Sr. It was nicknamed the "Snake Pit" because of all the wires and mikes hanging down. The mike and drums here were the ones used by Stevie Wonder.

The backdrop for the drums was put in place so they didn't overpower other instruments. The Steinway piano, built in 1877, was here since 1972. Sir Paul McCartney visited a few years ago. He tried to play it and found it way out of tune, he had it shipped to New York and had it retuned, but Gordy didn't want the outside changed. It was the instrument all of these stars played, and he wanted it to look the same.

There's a candy machine from the 1970s that tells a great story about one of Motown's biggest stars. Gordy instructed everyone at the studio that no one was to change the position of one candy,

Babe Ruths. That was because they were **Little Stevie Wonder**'s favorite candy. Other entertainers would often leave change on top of the machine and that little blind boy would go get his candy. This musical prodigy was born Stevland Hardaway Judkins on May 13, 1950. Due to his premature birth, he developed an eye condition in prenatal care that left him blind.

Little Stevie sang his own composition, "Lonely Boy" when he was just 11 to Ronnie White of the Miracles. White was so impressed he introduced the boy and his mother to Berry Gordy. Gordy was equally impressed and signed Stevie to a five-year contract. He also changed the child's stage name to Little Stevie Wonder.

When he was 12 years old, Stevie joined the Motortown Revue, touring the "Chitlin' Circuit." his 20-minute performance at the Regal Theater in Chicago was recorded and released in May 1963 as the album *Recorded Live: The 12-Year-Old Genius*. His single, from the album, "Fingertips," was also released in May, and became a number one hit on the Billboard Hot 100 when Wonder was just 13, making him the youngest artist ever to top the chart. It hit number one on the R&B chart simultaneously, another first for the child prodigy.

His talents were not limited to only one style of music; he had hits across the spectrum from R&B and jazz to pop and classical. He began to work in the Motown songwriting department, composing songs both for himself and his label mates. "The Tears of a Clown", a number one hit for Smokey Robinson and the Miracles, released in 1967 as the last track of their *Make It Happen* LP, but became a major success when re-released as a single in 1970, was his composition. Robinson repaid the favor when he co-wrote Stevie Wonder's, "Blame It on the Sun" for his 1972 album, "Talking Book."

Unlike many child prodigies, he continued a successful music career into the present. President Obama awarded him the Gershwin Prize in 2009 and Presidential Medal of Freedom in 2014. He received a Lifetime Achievement Award from the National Civil Rights Museum.

He is held in respect by fellow musicians. Wonder sang at the Michael Jackson memorial service in 2009, Etta James' funeral, in 2012, Whitney Houston's memorial service, and at Aretha Franklin's funeral in 2018.

(Top) Motown (Bottom) Motown studio

Chapter 18 Rock and Roll

Muddy Waters recorded the song, "The Blues Had a Baby and They Named It Rock and Roll." He doesn't mention the father, but you can bet on country. Some music historians credit July 5, 1954 as the day rock 'n' roll was born. It was the day a young singer with a fabulous smile and wiggly hips recorded "That's All Right Mama."

When Memphis radio WHBQ DJ, Dewey Philips, played the recording a few days later on July 8, most of the nation's teen-aged girls fell under the spell of the modest young man from Tupelo Mississippi who had moved to Memphis as a preteen. Other singers jumped on the bandwagon and Elvis's brand of rock and roll dominated the airways until the British invasion by four young men from Liverpool changed the style to a more international one. American music then became global. But Elvis was not alone in the evolution of rock and roll.

No question that rock and roll grew out of the blues and country. The question is where and how? Cleveland's Rock and Roll Hall of Fame is an amazing time travel trip into American music that helps answer that question. The Rock and Roll Hall of Fame in Cleveland, Ohio is one museum every music lover needs to visit. It's a must-see for any music lover. Sure, it's about rock and roll, but remember rock and roll evolved from blues and country with many other genres adding a touch or two. What I love about the museum is that it takes that into consideration and showcases those early influences. Over the years, they have inducted many influencers, including Sister Rosetta Tharpe, Ma Rainey, Robert Johnson, Hank Williams, Bob Willis, and countless other musician whose music led to rock and roll.

Rock and Roll Hall of Fame started in April 20, 1983 as an idea by Ahmet Ertegun and Jann Wenner, co-founders of Atlantic Records and Rolling Stone Magazine, respectively. It was just a concept originally and had its first class of inductees in 1986. Elvis Presley,

James Brown, Little Richard, Fats Domino, Ray Charles, Chuck Berry, Sam Cooke, the Everly Brothers, Buddy Holly, and Jerry Lee Lewis were inducted.

When they decided to open a museum, they considered many locations. Each had a unique connection to rock and roll. Cleveland won because of Alan Freed, a Cleveland disk jockey. In 1951, he was the first to call the style "Rock and Roll" on the radio. The unique pyramid style building designed by I.M. Pei, opened in 1995.

Jason Hanley, Vice President of Education and Visitor Engagement at the Rock and Roll Hall of Fame, and author of *We Rock!: A Fun Family Guide for Exploring Rock Music History*. Made a point that needs to be mentioned when you think of rock and roll. When we spoke of "the first rock and roll song," he said, "There isn't any."

I agree, since so many early songs had equal elements of what we consider rock and roll. Jason pointed out, "One of the earliest songs that has the words 'rock' and 'roll' in it is a blues song by Trixie Smith in 1922, 'My Man Rocks Me (With One Steady Roll).'"

You move from the roots of rock and roll, early blues, and country music, to Johnny Cash, Elvis and the Beetles. Exhibits showcase music as it evolved in different areas like Detroit, Muscle Shoals and other places where music made an impact.

One thing many of us have forgotten and younger people may not know about is told in the exhibit "Don't Knock the Rock." The exhibit has videos and artifacts telling how many politicians and preachers tried to stop rock and roll by calling it evil.

The second floor is the most interactive. Here you find The Garage where you can pick up an instrument and play or get together with friends and jam in a real studio with all the instruments.

The third floor is the holy grail, the Hall of Fame. Visit the Power of Rock Experience in the Connor Theater that showcases some highlights of induction ceremonies.

The Rock & Roll Hall of Fame held a groundbreaking on October 5, 2023 for its $135 million, 50,000 square-foot expansion project.

The museum will expand by one third, with the Main Exhibit Hall increasing to nearly 39,000 square feet. The additional room will allow the Rock Hall to hold larger traveling exhibits. They expect it to be completed by late 2025 or early 2026. The museum will remain open during construction.

A man with a terrific impact on the genre name is the reason the museum is in Cleveland. **Alan Freed** should be called "The High Priest of Rock and Roll" since he officially christened the music. As a young man he wanted to be a bandleader, but that didn't work out. He began as a disk jockey in Akron, Ohio and later moved to WJW radio, a major station in Cleveland, for a midnight program sponsored by Main Line, the RCA Distributor, and Record Rendezvous, a popular R&B record store. Freed had a hipper approach than the laid-back pop show DJs. In the early '50s, R&B records were played on lower-powered, inner city radio stations aimed at African-Americans. This was the first time that authentic R&B was featured regularly on a major radio station. Freed called his show "The Moondog House" and billed himself as "The King of the Moondoggers." He used a rhythm and blues record called "Moondog" as his theme song.

Freed wasn't the first to use the term, but he was the one who popularized it. The Boswell Sisters had a song called "Rock and Roll" they recorded in 1934, but it was typical jazz music. Billboard Magazine referred to it in a 1942 issue. Later, one of their columnists, Maurie Orodenker, used the term to describe upbeat recordings such as Sister Rosetta Tharpe's "Rock Me." But Alan Freed had the ear of white American teens who were listening for the first time to Black artists. Unlike other white DJs, Freed didn't play the cover versions; he played the originals by the black artists. He began using the term in the early '50s.

The term, and Freed, became very popular. Tapes of Freed's shows were played in New York. He appeared in several movies. In the 1956 film *Rock, Rock, Rock*, Freed tells the audience that "rock and roll is a river of music which has absorbed many streams: rhythm and blues, jazz, ragtime, cowboy songs, country songs, folk songs. All have contributed greatly to the big beat."

He helped organize and promote what is considered the first rock and roll concert, a show called "The Moondog Coronation Ball" on

March 21, 1952, at the Cleveland Arena. It was so well attended that the concert was shut down early due to overcrowding and a near-riot.

Freed later moved to New York and hosted on WINS Radio Station. Later, a conviction for tax evasion and bribery caused suspended sentence and fines and dulled his popularity. Like so many in the music field, his love of alcohol led to an early death on January 20, 1965. He was only 43. I visited his grave at Cleveland's Lake View Cemetery. If you go, look for the tombstone shaped like a jukebox.

In 1956, there was a TV show called *Bandstand,* hosted by Bob Horn. Horn was not appealing to the teens and pre-teens who WFIL-TV targeted for this show. The show's producers replaced him with a new, young radio host named **Dick Clark**. The show was renamed *American Bandstand*, and with Clark at its helm, became one of the most influential programs in the history of American music.

American Bandstand put **Chubby Checker** on top of the heap when he performed "The Twist," on the show in 1960. It became an instant hit and the new dance craze of American teens.

Hank Williams' first successful song, the 1947 blues rag "Move It On Over," done in the style he learned from Rufus "Tee Tot" Payne, a Black blues street musician, has music that is strikingly similar to Bill Haley and His Comets' "(We're Gonna) Rock Around the Clock," sometimes credited with birthing rock and roll to the masses a year after Williams died.

Rick Coleman, in his book, *Blue Monday: Fats Domino and the Lost Dawn of Rock 'n' Roll,* claims the first rock 'n' roll record was Fat's Domino's "The Fat Man" which hit #2 on the Billboard R&B chart in February 1950.

One of the country musicians playing in the earlier part of the twentieth century was guitarist **Jack Scott**. He was one of the first musicians to begin merging country into rock and roll with his Rockabilly Sound in the early 1950s.

"Rocket 88" recorded in March 1951, is the song usually credited with being the first rock and roll song. It's an unusual combination of blues and swing jazz, with a distorted sound caused by stuffing a broken guitar amplifier with wadded newspapers to hold it together, which unintentionally created the unusual sound. The vocal was Jackie Brenston, Ike Turner's saxophone player in his Kings of

Rhythm band. **Ike Turner** was unofficially the musician behind "Rocket 88" but the recording was credited "Jackie Brenston and His Delta Cats" because Sam Phillips, the producer, wanted to release a different record credited to Turner soon after. The song itself was a rewritten version of an old blues number, "Cadillac Boogie" by Jimmy Liggins. "Rocket 88" was released in April 1951 and remained No. 1 on the Billboard R&B chart for 5 weeks. Based on the date, it really was the first recorded rock and roll song.

Chuck Berry is sometimes called "The Father of Rock and Roll." His song "Maybellene," released in 1955, skillfully blends rhythm and blues with country. It was a changed version of an old county song, "Ida Red." He followed "Maybellene," which reached number 1 on Billboard magazine's rhythm and blues chart and number five on its Best Sellers in Stores chart for September 10, 1955, with a string of rock and roll hits. He released "Roll Over Beethoven" in 1956, "Rock and Roll Music" in 1957, and "Johnny B. Goode" in 1958. He appeared in two rock-and-roll movies: *Rock Rock Rock* and *Go, Johnny, Go*. He performed at the White House by invitation of President Jimmie Carter.

His career plummeted in December 1959 when he was arrested and subsequently convicted under the Mann Act. After his release, he rebounded somewhat. His 1972 song, "My Ding-a-Ling", a highly suggestive song for its time, went gold and hit number 1 in US, UK, and Canada.

He died in 2017 and is buried in Bellerive Gardens Cemetery, St. Louis. One good place to learn a lot about Chuck Berry is the National Blues Museum in his hometown of St. Louis. There's a statue of him in St. Louis at the Delmar Loop right across the street from Blueberry Hill Restaurant and Music Club. He has played over 200 concerts at Blueberry Hill. It's worth a visit, as it had tons of memorabilia related to Chuck Berry and rock and roll, plus great burgers.

The reason rock and roll became a worldwide phenomenon has to credit two men: Elvis Aaron Presley, the King of Rock and Roll, and Sam Phillips. According to music historian and journalist Peter Guralnick, Sam Phillips is "the man who invented Rock and Roll."

Sam Phillips grew up near Florence, Alabama. He describes his musical life in the 1920s and '30s in rural Alabama. "When I was growing up, we heard it all... In the fields we heard the black man's blues, in the churches we heard black spirituals and white gospel, and on the radio we heard the Grand Ole Opry... Out of that we created a sound that's hard to define, hard to pigeonhole, because it includes the best elements of all those tremendous sources,"

It was Sam's lifelong ambition to blend what was then called "race music," sung and listened to by only a Black audience, with country music white people heard. His quest led him to open Sun Studio, originally called Memphis Recording Services.

Mostly he recorded blues, his first love. One of his first discoveries was a man named Chester Burnett, better known by his stage name, Howlin' Wolf. Sam Phillips began to realize he needed to have his own label and began Sun Records in 1952 on the profits from "Rocket 88."

Sam was still hunting for that special sound. He found his answer in 1953 when a young truck driver came in to record a song called "My Happiness" supposedly for his mother's birthday. Sam's assistant, Marion Keisker, was impressed. She made a copy and played it for Sam, but he considered the song was just another conventional pop song. However, in 1954, he called the young man back to record again. Sam put him with a studio country band since the young singer had no band of his own. They tried a few country songs, but Sam didn't like the sound of any of those. But when the young singer, backed by Scotty Moore on guitar and Bill Black on bass, played around with a version of Arthur, "Big Boy" Crudup's 1949 blues song, "That's All Right Mamma," Sam loved it. He signed the singer to a three-year contract.

When Dewey Philips, DJ at WHBQ radio station, played the record on July eighth, that young singer, **Elvis Presley**, introduced rock and roll to the world. At least the white radio audience.

About a year and a half later, Sam sold Elvis's contract to RCA for around $35,000 because he was in financial trouble. Sam also recorded and helped springboard careers for Carl Perkins, Johnny Cash, Roy Orbison, Jerry Lee Lewis, and Charlie Rich. Sam Phillips was one of the first ten people inducted into the Rock 'n' Roll Hall of Fame in 1986, and was later inducted into the country, blues, and rockabilly Halls of Fame.

For a real thrill, visit Sun Studio in Memphis, now a museum. It is the high cathedral of rock and roll. Upstairs is a museum that shows you the history of the studio. One of my favorite exhibits is the actual WHBQ radio station booth Dewey Philips used when he played "That's All Right Mama." My biggest thrill was standing in that studio and singing in the same mike Elvis, Johnny Cash, and Jerry Lee used.

Even after RCA bought his contract, Elvis visited Sun Records. One December, Carl Perkins and Jerry Lee Lewis were recording. Johnny Cash was there also and the four friends had an impromptu jam session. Though Sun Records no longer had the right to release any of Elvis's material, Sam Phillips captured the session on tape. The results, released over 25 years later, became known as the "Million Dollar Quartet" recordings.

If you trace the factors that made Elvis Presley who he was, you start in Tupelo, Mississippi. Visit the small shotgun house where he was born. One of twins, his brother, Jesse, was stillborn. There is a lot of Elvis' story on the grounds, although he left there before he reached his teens when his family moved to Memphis. The birthplace has a Story Wall. On it, people who knew young Elvis have comments. One tells that Elvis knew music was in his future even then. Roland Tindall, a school friend, had this to say. "Elvis would pick his guitar and sing and tell us one day he was going to be on the Grand Ole Opry. We were all very doubtful of that, but we didn't say anything to him about it."

As a boy, Elvis' father changed jobs often, so they moved around Tupelo. He was first exposed to gospel music in Tupelo, where he attended Assembly of God Church with his parents. He often sang in the church choir. The church has been moved to the birthplace site. Another of the comments on the Story Wall is from his former pastor, Reverend Frank Smith, "His voice was a gift from God. Many have copied after him; he copied after nobody. His movements, his singing gyrations, those were his way. They didn't come from the church or other singers. He just kept at what he had begun in East Tupelo and did it his way."

But gospel and country weren't Elvis's only influences. As a youngster in Tupelo, the Presley family often lived in neighborhoods adjacent to African American communities. Elvis adsorbed the music he heard coming from those clubs and churches. Later, as a teen in Memphis, his family lived just a mile from Beale Street. It was no accident that his first hit was a blues song. The flip song was one made famous by Bob Wills, the bluegrass classic, "Blue Moon of Kentucky."

While you're in Tupelo, visit Tupelo Hardware. There is a bronze plaque on the storefront telling how Elvis's mother, Gladys, bought him his first guitar here. A lifelike cutout of Elvis greets you from the second-floor balcony.

For lunch, stop at Johnnie's Drive-In right across from his birthplace. They tout a fried banana and peanut butter sandwich as his favorite, but when we visited, we were told his favorite was the old-fashioned hamburger like mothers made at home in the years after WWII when families learned to stretch meat to go farther. My mom made a version too. It was ground beef with bread crumbs, chopped onions, bell pepper, celery, and an egg mixed in to hold it together. Shape a nice flat burger and fry it crisp. Serve it on a mayo coated bun with lettuce, tomatoes, and pickles.

He got a shot at performing at the Grand Ole Opry in October 1954, where he sang "Blue Moon of Kentucky." His rock 'n' roll style wasn't a good fit with the traditional country crowd. In November that year, he joined the Louisiana Hayride and was more accepted. On March 3, 1955, he had his first television appearance on the television version of The Louisiana Hayride.

If you want to walk in the footsteps of Elvis Presley, Hank Williams, Sr., Johnny Cash and many other Country Music greats, take a backstage tour of the Shreveport Municipal Auditorium, former home of The Louisiana Hayride. Elvis's bronze statue stands in front with James Burton, one-time member of Elvis's band. Inside you'll find pictures of Elvis and of others who performed there and a copy of Elvis's Hayride contract. You can visit the dressing room Elvis used at the Hayride and learn how the phrase "Elvis has left the building" came about here.

Blues continued in Elvis's later records. Each of his next four records with Sun had a blues B side; "Good Rockin' Tonight," "Milk Cow Blues Boogie," "Baby, Let's Play House," and "Mystery Train." When he moved to RCA, his "Hound Dog," the flip side of "Don't be Cruel," had been a blues hit for Big Mama Thornton. Elvis's version did much better. Elvis's 1956 "Don't Be Cruel/Hound Dog" is one of just two records where both sides have, separately, been voted into the Grammy Hall of Fame. It also set a rock-era record until 1992 ranking number one for 11 weeks.

Elvis's post stardom life is reflected in Graceland, the Southern colonial mansion on a 13.8 acre estate on the outskirts of Memphis. He bought it in the spring of 1957, and moved his parent and grandmother in to the home. Elvis now had played in two Hollywood movies, *Love Me Tender* and *Loving You*. He had released two studio albums and 48 singles and was such a megastar he needed a place where he had a semblance of privacy from his millions of fans. In 1991, it was named to the National Register of Historic Places.

The den, where he and his family and friends relaxed and watched television, is named "the Jungle Room" because of its exotic decor. Even the ceiling is green shag carpet.

He was reaching an audience outside of the county, blues, and rock and roll genera. "Heartbreak Hotel" became Presley's first number-one pop hit. More conservative media and many religious leaders denounced him for his pelvic rotations on stage, claiming it was inflaming young minds. He earned the nickname "Elvis the Pelvis."

One example of those reactions occurred at the Florida Theater in Jacksonville. Elvis was almost arrested here at his second performance in 1956. At his first performance, the year before, teen girls almost tore his clothes off as he exited the theater. This time a juvenile court judge, appropriately named Judge Gooding, decided there would be no more such lascivious behavior.

Gooding issued a warrant and informed Elvis before the show, if he did any "dirty moves" he'd be arrested. The judge attended the show and sat in the first row with his young daughter to insure his orders were obeyed. Elvis stood behind the piano. Lower seats saw him from the waist up. Balcony seats got a full-frontal view. He performed as usual, however the judge, in his lower front row seat, saw nothing improper. Elvis wasn't arrested. The girls mobbed Elvis as he left as usual.

As he focused more on movies and doing soundtracks, his popularity and wealth grew. He loved automobiles and purchased many. Twenty-two of his cars are displayed at Graceland Plaza, directly across from Graceland in the Elvis Presley Automobile Museum. You'll find his 1955 pink Cadillac, his 1956 purple Cadillac convertible, his 1973 Stutz Blackhawk, and some of his motorcycles.

For commuting between Hollywood and Memphis, he bought two jet planes, the first named the *Hound Dog II* and the larger, later one he named the *Lisa Marie*, after his daughter. There is a "Sincerely, Elvis," exhibit there that has many of his clothing and personal items.

Drafted into the army in 1954 as he was finishing filming, *King Creole* slowed his career for a short time. When he was discharged in March 1960, he cut the album, *Elvis Is Back!*, for RCA and resumed performing. The Colonel pushed Elvis into musical movies with songs, most of which he disliked.

He married Priscilla Beaulieu on May 1, 1967. Their only child, Lisa Marie, was born on February 1, 1968; she died Jan. 12, 2023. The marriage failed and their divorce was finalized on October 9, 1973. Meanwhile, in spite of his outspoken condemnation of "drug culture" and even having received an honorary badge from President Nixon as a member of the Bureau of Narcotics and Dangerous Drugs, he became addicted to prescription drugs. His earliest abuse began in the army. By the time of his death he was a long-time abuser, not only of amphetamines, but of opiates, antihistamines, and tranquilizers, barbiturates, Quaaludes, sleeping pills, hormones, and laxatives, for the constipation caused by overuse of opioids. He was suffering from chronic constipation, diabetes, and glaucoma. Bodyguards and friends who worked with him saw the damage occurring and tried to suggest getting help. The Colonel instead fired anyone who suggested Elvis had a problem. His personal physician gave him whatever he wanted.

He was only 42 when he died on August 16, 1977. I remember the day I heard it announced on the car radio. I was living in Mississippi and driving to pick up my kids from the Buccaneer Park swimming pool. He and his parents are buried in the Meditation garden at Graceland.

Elvis was inducted into the Rock and Roll of Fame in Cleveland, Ohio, in 1986, its first batch of inductees, before the museum even had a building. His exhibit is updated every two years with loaned items from Graceland. It's worth a visit for any rock and roll fan. Not only is Elvis enshrined there, but all the legends of rock and roll.

Another contender for earliest rock and roll is **Bill Haley** and the Comets' release of "Rock Around the Clock" on April 1954, about two months before Elvis's record. However, it didn't make much of an impression, barely making number 23 on the Billboard pop singles chart. When he re-released it in 1955, as the theme song of the 1955 film *Blackboard Jungle*, the record soared to number one on the American Billboard chart and stayed on the chart for eight weeks. He followed it up with "Shake, Rattle and Roll." It was originally a rhythm and blues song by Big Joe Turner. Haley speeded it up with some Western swing and changed some lyrics. The record went on to sell a million copies and was the first rock and roll song to place on the UK Singles Chart. In 1956, he released "See You Later, Alligator" which became a standard parting comment in the '50s. When a departing friend said, "See You Later, Alligator" it was routinely answered with the second part of the chorus, "After while Crocodile," The same year he played in two movies, *Rock Around the Clock* and *Don't Knock the Rock*.

He was born William John Clifton Haley in Detroit's Highland Park July 6, 1925, and died February 9, 1981 in his home at Harlingen, Texas.

Since I came of age listening to **Jerry Lee Lewis**, AKA The Killer, pounding a piano and belting out his hits, I jumped at the chance to visit Ferriday, Louisiana, where he was born on September 29, 1935. Ferriday is somewhat of a musical hotspot since the tiny town was the birthplace of Jerry Lee Lewis and his cousin, Mickey Gilley. When I entered Delta Music Museum, the town's three most famous residents were there to greet me. Mickey Gilley and Jimmy Swaggart stood by the piano as Jerry Lee pounded the keys. Well, actually, they were life-sized mannequins, but you get the feeling they are there in spirit. It's also the Delta Music Hall of Fame. The Delta Music Museum filled with information and artifacts from famous Louisiana musicians from the singing governor, Jimmy Davis, whose horse, Sunshine, inspired what is now Louisiana's State Song, "You are My Sunshine" and how Jerry Lee earned the nickname "Killer,"

According to a docent, Jerry Lee failed seventh grade. When he returned to school the next year, he wanted to be in the same class as his friends, so he just went to that classroom. When the teacher told him to return to the 7th grade class, he grabbed the teacher by his tie and was choking him until one of Jerry Lee's friends pulled him away from the gasping teacher.

Throughout his outrageous and sometimes scandalous, but usually successful, career, he lived up to the youthful nickname. His rocking slamming piano style created hits like "Whole Lotta Shakin' Goin' On" and "Great Balls of Fire." He almost destroyed that career when it became known he had married his 13-year-old cousin Myra Brown Williams. Myra was nine years Jerry Lee's junior when they eloped. Making it even stranger, his divorce to his second wife had not been finalized. Jerry Lee and Myra remarried and had two children before she filed for divorce for physical and mental abuse.

He moved on to record county songs, many of which became hits over his seven-decade career. Jerry Lee had 30 songs reach the Top 10 on the Billboard Country and Western Chart including "To Make Love Sweeter for You," "There Must Be More to Love Than This," "Would You Take Another Chance on Me," and "Me and Bobby McGee."

Jerry Lee passed away on October 28, 2022, at his home in Hernando County, Mississippi. His seventh wife, Judith Brown, sort of brought his marriages full-circle in the odd department. She was the former wife of Myra's brother.

Over his lifetime, he recorded a dozen gold records in rock and roll and country. He won four Grammy Awards, including a Lifetime Achievement Award and two Hall of Fame Awards. He was inducted into the Rock and Roll Hall of Fame in 1986 the Country Music Hall of Fame in 2022.

One highlight of my teen years was seeing Jerry Lee Lewis perform at what is now Louis Armstrong Auditorium. In those days, parents could come into the auditorium and pick up their children from shows. I remember my dad, a product of the big band era, coming to pick me up and seeing the look on his face when he saw Jerry Lee jumping up and down and pounding on that piano.

Little Richard was born Richard Wayne Penniman in Macon, Georgia on December 5, 1932. He earned the name Little Richard as a child because of his slim, effeminate build. He was one of the most influential figures in early rock and roll and is called the "Architect of Rock and Roll." His life and music career careened between his early fundamentalist upbringing in segregated Georgia and his sexual identity. His biggest hits are legends of rock and roll "Tutti Frutti," "Long Tall Sally," and "Good Golly, Miss Molly,"

He got his start at Ann's Tic Toc Lounge, a restaurant and nightclub owned by Ann Howard. It was one of Macon's first openly gay bars; a place where Black or white, gay or straight were welcome. Little Richard worked there as a dishwasher when he was a teenager. Miss Ann let him perform when he wasn't bussing tables. Sadly, due to a fire Tic Toc is now closed down.

He was one of the first batch of inductees into the Rock and Roll Hall of Fame in 1986. He was also inducted into the Songwriters Hall of Fame and is the recipient of Lifetime Achievement Awards from The Recording Academy and the Rhythm and Blues Foundation. Richard received a Rhapsody & Rhythm Award from the National Museum of African American Music In 2015, for his part in the formation of popular music genres that helped end the racial divide on the music charts and in concert. "Tutti Frutti" was included in the National Recording Registry of the Library of Congress in 2010, because of his "unique vocalizing over the irresistible beat announced a new era in music."

Little Richard was a familiar figure on Macon's streets. Alan Walden told the story about his older brother, Phil Walden, who was just a teenager at the time but later founder Phil Walden Artists and Promotions, the company that managed Otis Redding. Later Walden was co-founder of Capricorn Records in Macon. Phil was walking on a sidewalk in downtown Macon and saw Little Richard coming from the opposite direction on the sidewalk across the street, wearing a red suit with a matching parasol. Too star-struck to speak until Richard had passed, Phil called out to his back, "Tootie Fruitti!" To which Richard stopped, looked over his shoulder, and replied, "Good bootie!" with a shake of his own.

Late in his career, Richard denounced his music and his homosexuality and became an evangelist. When he returned to the music world, in October 1962, the Beatles were his opening act.

He again returned to the church, evangelism, and selling Bibles. He stopped performing for a time, but he once again returned to his music in 1986. Little Richard was inducted into the Rock and Roll Hall of Fame, and appeared in the movie "Down and Out in Beverly Hills." His "Great Gosh A'Mighty," from the movie soundtrack, even put him back on the charts for the first time in more than 15 years.

When you visit Macon, be sure to tour the recently reopened Capricorn Studio and its museum. Macon honors her native son at the Tubman Museum of African-American Art, History, and Culture. There are extensive music exhibits there about other Georgia musicians, as well as Little Richard.

Antoine Domino, Jr.'s boogie-woogie piano playing rooted in blues, rhythm & blues, and jazz, made him one of the early pioneers of rock and roll. He was born in New Orleans on February 26, 1928, and earned the name that is known worldwide when Billy Diamond, a local bandleader and bass player, who invited him to play in his band at the Hideaway Club in New Orleans, nicknamed him **"Fats" Domino** after Fats Waller, another famous piano player.

Fats got bitten by the music bug early. When his sister, Philones, married Harrison Verrett, a New Orleans banjo player, who taught his young brother-in-law how to play piano, that became young Antoine's passion. He quit school when he was 14 and went to work in Crescent City Bed Factory by day and performed in Ninth Ward clubs at night.

Fats began working with Dave Bartholomew, a producer, songwriter, and bandleader, who co-wrote and produced many of Domino's hits including his first record, "The Fat Man," which hit #1 on the February 1950 R&B charts. "The Fat Man" is often cited as one of the first rock and roll records.

For the next five years, Fats Domino and Bartholomew's band recorded a steady stream of hits for Imperial Records. Domino's 1955 "Ain't That a Shame" was covered by Pat Boone, who also covered many of Little Richard and other rock and roll style songs. Some of Domino's biggest hits include "I'm in Love Again," "Blueberry Hill," "Blue Monday," and "Walking to New Orleans." Over the years, he accumulated 23 gold singles and 37 Billboard Top 40 hits.

By the end of 1956, Fats was making appearances on major network television and was in several Hollywood films; *The Girl Can't Help It* and *Shake, Rattle and Rock*. He appeared as himself in several episodes of the TV series, *Treme*.

When you're in New Orleans, you can see Fats Domino's Grand Piano at the Presbyter just as it was found after Hurricane Katrina. It headlines the exhibit "Living with Hurricanes: Katrina and Beyond." Another of his pianos, a white Steinway, anchors the "Louisiana Jukebox" exhibit at the Old Mint. Fats Domino's heritage is so important that the Rock and Roll Hall of Fame and Paul McCartney contributed to restoring his piano.

Fats Domino was a true New Orleanian who never left his roots. You would see him driving around the city in his trademark pink Cadillac.

Growing up in New Orleans, he was one of my music staples. I loved seeing his home as we drove over the Industrial Canal Bridge on Claiborne Avenue. He remained in that shotgun double with yellow trimmed roofline until Hurricane Karina drove him out. The street in front has been renamed Fats Domino Avenue.

Bo Diddley's real name Ellas Otha Bates McDaniel, is credited with popularizing the "Bo Diddley beat", a syncopated rhythm often used in rock and roll music. Diddley's music is often classified as rhythm and blues, but it also has elements of blues, rock and roll, and even country music, and many aspects of present day hip-hop music. He was a master of the electric guitar and his music was often characterized by his distinctive guitar sound and his energetic live performances. He added many technical innovations to his music to enhance the sound of his custom-made rectangular-shaped guitars.

Some of his most notable hits include: "Bo Diddley," "I'm a Man," "Who Do You Love?," "Sixty Minute Man," and "Mona."

Bo Diddley is remembered in Gainesville, Florida. Archer, where he lived until his death in 2008, is part of the Gainesville Metropolis area. Matherson History Museum, a small free museum, features exhibits about Bo Diddley. The main hall features "Return to Forever: Gainesville's Great Southern Music Hall." Between 1974 and 1978 this was Gainesville's top concert venue, Great Southern Music Hall, located in the historic Florida Theatre, hosted Bo Diddley and many other music legends including Muddy Waters, Jimmy Buffett, Bob Seger, Ray Charles, Steve Martin, Ike and Tina Turner, the Count Basie Orchestra, and many more.

Bo Diddley Community Plaza in Historic Downtown Gainesville was named in his honor in 2008. The plaza hosts concerts and festivals throughout the year.

Early rock and roll doesn't abound in female singers. Yes, there were many great female singers during the mid-'50s to mid-'60s. Most fall into the rhythm and blues or country category even though their music ranked on the rock and roll charts, like Aretha Franklin or Brenda Lee.

Tina Turner earned the title, "Queen of Rock 'n' Roll," first as the lead singer of the Ike & Tina Turner Revue and later as a solo performer. She began singing with the group in 1957 under the name Little Ann. They married in 1962; divorced in 1978, when Tina could take no more of his abuse. Ike Turner might have been a pioneer in rock and roll, but he was a louse as a husband.

After her divorce, she re-launched her solo career in the 1980s. Her 1984 multi-platinum album *Private Dancer* with the song "What's Love Got to Do with It", won the Grammy Award for Record of the Year and became her first and only number-one song on the Billboard Hot 100. During her Break Every Rule World Tour in 1988, she broke the then Guinness World Record for the largest paying audience, 180,000 tickets, for a solo performer.

She retired in 2009, after completing her Tina!: 50th Anniversary Tour, the 15th-highest-grossing tour of the 2000s. Turner acted in the films *Tommy* in 1975 and *Mad Max Beyond Thunderdome* in

1985. Her autobiography *I, Tina: My Life Story,* was adapted for the 1993 film *What's Love Got to Do with It.* In 2018, *Tina*, a jukebox musical with Adrienne Warren playing Tina, debuted.

Over her lifetime, she sold more than 100 million records worldwide, making her one of the best-selling recording artists of all time. She received 12 Grammy Awards. Tina was the first black artist and first woman to be on the cover of *Rolling Stone* that ranked her among the 100 Greatest Artists of All Time and the 100 Greatest Singers of All Time. She was inducted into the Rock and Roll Hall of Fame twice, with Ike Turner in 1991 and as a solo artist in 2021. Tina was also a 2005 recipient of the Kennedy Center Honors and Women of the Year award.

West Tennessee Delta Heritage Center in Brownsville is the place to visit to learn about Tina Turner, and as a bonus, lots of other West Tennessee musicians like "Sleepy John" Estes from Brownsville, Tennessee and his band members; James "Yank" Rachell, a guitarist and mandolin player, and Hammie Nixon, a harmonica player. They were known as the Brownsville Bluesmen. I never knew Carl Perkins, who recorded the original version of "Blue Suede Shoes," and country star, Eddie Arnold, were also from West Tennessee.

When I ventured out behind the museum, I struck musical gold again. I was thrilled to explore "Sleepy" John Estes Home and The Flagg Grove School where Tina Turner attended school. The school was sitting in an old field, deteriorating. Tina's grandfather built the old school. Sonia Outlaw-Clark, the center director, and a group of local citizens gained possession of the school house and brought it on the Heritage Center grounds in 2012. That year's annual Tina Turner Heritage Days, held each year on the fourth weekend in September, was a big success.

The school house was restored and officially opened for "Tina Turner Heritage Days" that year. Sonia told me how much Tina helped make this newest exhibit a success. "She (Tina) contributed financially and with memorabilia, gold records and costumes. Even her yearbook. They are all on display.

"Tina even sent her personal assistant, Rhonda Graam, to help. When Rhonda visited she had never been here before. We traveled all over Nutbush. Tina had sent a whole list of places 'I want to know if this is still there. I want to know what's here'"

The school is set up to show what it was like going to an African American school in the 1940s and 50s.

When I heard on the news on May 24, 2023, that Tina Turner had passed away, I felt I had lost a friend. Her "Proud Mary" in on my Spotify list all the time.

Janis Joplin might be considered rock and roll's last great female star. Born in Port Arthur, Texas on Jan. 19, 1943. Janis Joplin has been called "The Queen of Rock" and "The Queen of Psychedelic Soul," but her style is uniquely her own. She joined Big Brother and the Holding Company. Big Brother's second album, "Cheap Thrills" included the hits "Piece of My Heart" and "Summertime" ranked No. 1 on the Billboard 200 and sold over a million copies in the first month. It was certified gold on October 15, 1968. Joplin split with Big Brother and formed the Kozmic Blues Band with whom she performed at Woodstock in 1969. She later created the Full Tilt Boogie Band in 1970. On October 4, 1970, Joplin died from a heroin overdose. Three days earlier, she had recorded her last song, "Mercedes Benz."

A replica of Joplin's psychedelic 1965 Porsche 356 Cabriolet can be seen at the Museum of the Gulf Coast, which has an extensive music wing featuring Joplin and many other stars.

There is a bust of the **Big Bopper**, **Buddy Holly**, and **Ritchie Valens** commemorating their death in a plane crash. On Feb. 3, 1959, rock stars Buddy Holly, J.P. "The Big Bopper" Richardson, and Ritchie Valens were killed when their plane crashed in Iowa. Buddy Holly and his band, consisting of Waylon Jennings, Tommy Allsup, and Carl Bunch, were playing on the "Winter Dance Party" tour across the Midwest along with Valens, Richardson, and vocal group Dion and the Belmonts. The long journeys between venues on a cold, cramped tour bus was something every performer tried to avoid.

Ironically, one of Holly's first hits, "That'll be the day", refers to the day he dies, althought it was overshadowed by his bigger hit, "Peggy Sue."

It was due to a simple act of kindness that Waylon was not on that plane. He gave up his seat on the plane to the Big Bopper, J.P.

Richardson, because Richardson, a large man who was suffering with a cold or flu at the time and hated being confined in a small bus for long periods.

The Big Bopper was also an inspired songwriter. He wrote "Running Bear," the story of an ill-fated love affair between a man and woman from rival tribes, for Johnny Preston, another Port Arthur musician. Richardson grew up along the Sabine River and recalled stories about local Indian tribes. Preston's recording was released August 1959, six months after Richardson's death, and became a No. 1 hit for three weeks in January 1960. His own "Chantilly Lace," had just gone gold, but he never got to receive his gold record.

Valens was creating Chicano rock. He had recently had a big hit with his "La Bamba" adapted from a Mexican folk song. He was not supposed to be on the plane, but won his seat on a coin toss with Allsup. The incident became known as "the day the music died" in 1971 when the tragedy inspired **Don Mclean** to write "American Pie."

Visitors to the museum can view *Southern Discomfort*, a documentary about the life of Janis Joplin, in the Museum's Lloyd Hayes Theater. The museum suggests that visitors schedule film screenings in advance by calling 409-982-7000.

Joplin was inducted into the Rock and Roll Hall of Fame in 1995, and awarded a Grammy Lifetime Achievement Award in 2005. She also has a star on the Hollywood Walk of Fame.

Another local musician the museum is very proud of is George Jones. He was born in Saratoga, Texas. In 1942, the Jones family moved to a government-subsidized housing project in Beaumont.

Maurice Woodward Ritter, known in the country music and movie world as "Tex" was born in Panola County, Texas. Ritter moved to Nederland, Texas as a child. Tex Ritter Park in Nederland just outside Port Arthur has some great exhibits about him. This museum is a treasure for music history and more.

Another place to find more about not only Tex Ritter but Texas music in general is The Texas Country Music Hall of Fame/Tex Ritter Museum in Carthage, Texas. The museum also features other Texas-born country music legends. In August 2004, the museum added a Jim Reeves display which features the radio equipment from Jim's radio station KGRI in Henderson.

Jimi Hendrix was one of the leading musicians, as rock and roll morphed into harder versions of rock. Hendrix was influenced by blues singers and began as a R&B musician but soon became know for his psychedelic rock. He played clubs in New York and later England, but what brought him into the public eye was when he played the 1967 Monterey Pop Festival where he went down in rock history when he burned his guitar. According to Hendrix, "I decided to destroy my guitar at the end of a song as a sacrifice. You sacrifice things you love. I love my guitar." It made a pretty good publicity act, too.

His biggest hit song was "Purple Haze," about a girl so bewitching him he was in a purple haze. He was known for his unique and innovative sound effects in his guitar playing. *Rolling Stone* ranked his albums, *Are You Experienced* (1967), *Axis: Bold as Love* (1967), and *Electric Ladyland* (1968) among the 500 Greatest Albums of All Time and ranked Hendrix number six on their list of the 100 greatest artists of all time, and number one on their list of the 100 greatest guitarists of all time. He died far too young at the age of 27 from a drug overdose.

For those of us of a certain age, Memphis, with its musical heritage, is like a pilgrimage. After you've visited Beale Street, Graceland, and Sun Studio, take a tour of Memphis Rock and Soul Museum. John Doyle, executive director, explained why Rock and Soul Museum is so important in telling the history of Rock and Roll. "We are the only museum that is a full standing museum outside of D.C. that isn't owned by but is totally researched and curated by the Smithsonian. Kind of a cool story. They were doing a couple of research projects tracing the history of rock and soul which they maintained were two true American genres of music."

Rock and Soul Museum offers an audiovisual tour where you put on a headset and listen to the stories of how these two forms morphed into a new and explosive sound. The museum is extensive and tracks music from the early days of sharecroppers to the present. Follow Ike Turner in 1951 as he records "Rocket 88." See how a young Elvis was influenced by the Black musicians of the time.

The British Invasion occurred in February 1964, when the Beetles, took the nation by storm appearing on The Ed Sullivan show. "I Want to Hold Your Hand" hit the top of just about every music chart. In a way it was the end of a completely American music. Music was now global.

Many different versions of rock came into being in the 70s; punk rock, psychedelic rock, heavy metal, alternative rock, even disco.

Long live rock and roll!

Elvis exhibit at Cleveland Rock and Roll Hall of Fame

*(Top) Author holding same mike used by Elvis, Johnny Cash, Jerry Lee Lewis and other musicians at Sun Studio in Memphis
(Bottom) Graceland, Elvis's home in Memphis*

Statue of young Elvis at his boyhood home in Tupelo, MS

(Top) Tanya Tucker's schoolhouse at the West Tennessee Delta Heritage in Brownsville, TN (Bottom) Display of musicians who played there including, Elvis, Johnny Cash, and more at Shreveport Auditorium

*(Top)Janis Joplin's car at Museum of the Gulf Coast in Port Arthur, TX
(Bottom) Fats Domino's Piano at the Presbytere, New Orleans*

*(Top) Chuck Berry exhibit at Rock and Roll Hall of fame, Cleveland, OH
(Bottom) Chuck Berry statue in St. Louis, MO*

Chapter 19 Folk Music and Protest Era

Protest in song have been going on for a long time. Music historians attribute the first protest song recorded to Billie Holiday, who recorded her iconic version of "Strange Fruit" on April 20, 1939. It dealt with lynching and Black bodies hanging from trees. Even before that, enslaved people sang old biblical songs that were meant as a protest against their masters and the system.

In the 1940s, Josh White, one of the first musicians to make a name for himself singing against Jim Crow laws. Undoubtedly, a personal tragedy when he was still a child in 1921 was a big influence on his music. A white bill collector who came to his family's home became aggressive and spit on the floor. White's father pushed the bill collector out the door. The man returned that night with law officers. They arrested, beat, and dragged his father tied behind a horse. His father was mentally and physically injured and spent the rest of his life in a mental institution. He died in 1930 due to the injuries.

As a black musician, White had the ear of President Roosevelt. Franklin and Eleanor Roosevelt were both fans of folk music. White had a friendly relationship with the first family. His first protest album, *Joshua White & His Carolinians: Chain Gang*, released by Columbia Records in 1940, included the song "Trouble", which told about why he had always been in trouble because he was a black-skinned man. The album was played on white radio stations and sold in Southern record stores. It caused outrage among many racists.

To show their support, Eleanor Roosevelt invited White and the band he was currently leading, the Golden Gate Quartet, to perform at a concert celebrating the 75th Anniversary of the Thirteenth Amendment at the Library of Congress's Coolidge Auditorium on December 20, 1940. In January 1941, White performed in Washington again at the President's Inauguration. In March 1941 he released the album, *Southern Exposure*, with six anti-segregationist songs including "Southern Exposure," "Hard Time Blues," and "Jim Crown Train."

White also sang on the Almanac Singers' anti peace-time draft album, *Songs for John Doe*. Despite this, in 1941, President Roosevelt invited White to become the first African American artist to give a White House Command Performance.

During the McCarthy era, he was forced to testify before the House Committee on Un-American Activity. Despite his avowal that he stood for democracy and equal rights for all, he was blackballed. He and his wife relocated to Europe until 1954.

He made somewhat of a comeback in 1963 when President Kennedy, also a folk music fan, invited White to appear on a CBS-TV special. White also marched and performed on Dr. Martin Luther King Jr.'s March on Washington.

Pete Seeger was another folk singer who fell into the clutches of McCarthyism. He was a strong supporter of labor unions. In 1936, when he was 17, he joined the Young Communist League (YCL). From 1942 to 1949, he was a member of the Communist Party USA. Seeger performed with the Almanac Singers who were critical of Roosevelt's 1940 peacetime draft order, and later The Weavers. The group was pro-union, opposed segregation, and anti-semitism. Seeger and The Almanacs were joined by Woody Guthrie and other like-minded musicians on *Songs for John Doe* and *Talking Union* both released in 1941.

In *Songs for John Doe,* they promote the theory that the US was about to get into the war to help big businesses who produced arms and other wartime materials. There are lyrics about it not being much of a thrill to be killed in Brazil fighting for DuPont.

"Talking Union," the title song for that album, sung by Seeger, is a talking blues song that tells how to organize a union. Josh White and Woody Guthrie are also on that album.

However, their stance on draft and war changed when Germany broke the non-aggression pact, and invaded the Soviet Union, and even more so after the Japanese bombed Pearl Harbor.

They pulled *Songs for John Doe* off the market and asked anyone with a copy to return it. (Note if you find an original copy at a flea market or garage sale, grab it. A good condition copy of the album can typically sell for between $500 and $1,000 but beware of counterfeits.)

Seeger and the Almanacs recorded *Dear Mr. President*, an album in support of Roosevelt and the war effort. In the title song, "Dear Mr. President," Seeger sings a solo by telling President Roosevelt that, although they didn't agree in the past about segregation and labor conditions, winning this war and stopping Hitler was the most important thing now.

Seeger put his money where his mouth was and, when drafted into the army in 1942, served honorably in Special Services.

After the war and the news of the atomic bombings of Hiroshima and Nagasaki, many people feared a nuclear war.

Seeger recorded one of the first nuclear protest songs, "Talking Atom," in 1948. "Talking Atom" was written by Vern Partlow as "Old Man Atom." The song used well-known lines with a slight change like "We hold these truths to be self-evident/All men may be created equal" and substituted the word "cremated" for "created." It didn't go over well with Joe McCarthy.

The House on Un-American Activities Committee subpoenaed Seeger in 1955. Even though he knew about the 1950 conviction and imprisonment of the Hollywood Ten for contempt of Congress, Seeger refused to plead the Fifth Amendment. He refused to name personal and political associations on the grounds that this violated First Amendment rights: "I am not going to answer any questions as to my association, my philosophical or religious beliefs or my political beliefs, or how I voted in any election." They found him guilty of contempt of Congress in March 1961. He was sentenced to ten one-year simultaneous terms in jail, but an appeals court overturned his conviction in May 1962.

Government harassment didn't stop Seeger from his protest music. Seeger's anti-war songs, such as "Where Have All the Flowers Gone?" co-written with Joe Hickerson who added the last few verses to make it a circular song start with questioning the disappearance of all the flowers in a cemetery picked by the young girls. Each later voice takes it a step further, asking where all the young girls have gone? Answering that they have married young men. Then each verse in turn tells that the young men become soldiers, then graves, then return to the flowers. If you haven't heard it, find it online and listen. It is one of the most moving songs, and yet so simple in its explanations. Seeger recorded an abbreviated version in 1960 and then a full version in 1964. It was covered by The Kingston Trio, Peter Paul and Mary, Joan Baez, and pretty much all the protest singers and others. Pete Seeger's recording of his composition was inducted into the Grammy Hall of Fame, which is a special Grammy Award established in 1973 to honor recordings that are at least 25 years old and that have "qualitative or historical significance."

In 1963, he helped organize a Carnegie Hall concert for the young Freedom Singers. The same year, he joined the March on Washington for Jobs and Freedom in August singing "We Shall Overcome." He sang it again on the Selma to Montgomery, Alabama march. On his 1966 album *Dangerous Songs!?,* Seeger sent a not-too-veiled message to end the Vietnam War to President Lyndon Johnson with his recording of Len Chandler's children's song "Beans in My Ears." Seeger added a verse where he claims Mrs. Jay's son Alby had "beans in his ears." It was easy to convert "Alby Jay" to Johnson's nickname "LBJ" and say he did not listen to anti-war protests as he had "beans in his ears."

Seeger, along with Malvina Reynolds, released one of the first environmental albums, *God Bless the Grass,* in 1966.

Seeger waded deeper into the anti-Vietnam-War protest in 1967 with his song "Waist Deep in the Big Muddy." A song about a captain believed to be a big fool who drowned while leading a platoon into danger on maneuvers in Louisiana during World War II. With its lyrics about a platoon being led into danger by an ignorant captain, the song's anti-war message was obvious, and it is clear he is referring to LBJ as "the fool." The odd thing was he performed it on a comedy show, the Smothers' Brothers show, on February 25, 1968.

His anti-Vietnam-War push continued on November 15, 1969, when he led 500,000 protesters in singing John Lennon's song "Give Peace a Chance" in the Vietnam Moratorium March on Washington, DC.

Like Woody Guthrie's guitar with a sticker saying "This machine kills fascists," Seeger's banjo was adorned with the motto "This Machine Surrounds Hate and Forces It to Surrender."

Seeger's musical accomplishments continued when he invented the long-neck or Seeger banjo that is three frets longer than a typical banjo, and slightly longer than a bass guitar at 25 frets.

Folk artists such as **Woody Guthrie**, Josh White, and Pete Seeger had many plenty of merging genres in their songs. The melody of "This Land is Your Land," by Woody Guthrie has a lot of similarity to a gospel song by Carter Family "When the World's on Fire." The lyrics are quite different. In fact, the lyrics changed between 1940 when Guthrie, an outspoken protester for social justice and the right of the common man, wrote the first version and when he recorded it in 1944. It was released in 1949 by a small company called Folkways Recording Company. In the later version, he omits the verses about greedy capitalism that were in the 1940 version. This was the time of McCarthyism when even a hint of Socialistic beliefs got writers, actors, and others blackballed or even jailed as "Communists," which probably explains the changes. He changed the title from his original "God Blessed America For Me" to "This Land is Your Land."

> As I went walking I saw a sign there
> And on the sign it said "No Trespassing."
> But on the other side it didn't say nothing,
> That side was made for you and me.
>
> In the shadow of the steeple I saw my people,
> By the relief office I seen my people;
> As they stood there hungry, I stood there asking
> Is this land made for you and me?

Arlo Guthrie carried on in his father's footsteps with his "Alice's Restaurant," a satirical protest against the Vietnam War. The song is 18 minute 34 second long; the same span of time as one of the gaps in Nixon's Watergate tapes. When he sang at Woodstock, he didn't do any protest songs.

In the mid '60s and early '70s and into the 1980s protest songs became so popular they rate a genre of their own. Two major factors influenced this era: the Vietnam War and Civil Rights. Both became much broader issues and changed society. A cultural change was occurring at the same time. Young people growing up under the constant threat of the Cold War exploding into a nuclear disaster began to question their depression era parent's idea of the American Dream. The Hippie Era was influenced less by material wealth than by being happy and free of worry. A natural idea when you grew up seeing the Korean War, originally a civil war between North and South Korean factions which escalated into a proxy war between the Soviet Union and its allies and the US and its western allies, which lasted from 1950 to 1953 and the ongoing Cold War. In the '50s we had "Bomb Drills" supposedly to help us protect ourselves from a nuclear attack by Russia. We were told to duck under our desks and cover our heads with our hands. Yeah! That was going to do a lot of good against an atomic bomb. Vietnam was the last straw.

Hippies took the values of the former Beatniks and ran with them. Make love, not war! "Turn on, tune in, and drop out." "Sex, drugs, and rock 'n' roll." "Hell no, we won't go." Since Hippies were apolitical, the protest was almost an accidental result. Yet, becoming involved in another civil war far away, was part of what drove the movement, protest songs and hippie culture were intertwined. Plus Hippies believed in Mother Earth, equality for all, sexual freedom, and above all, peace. The music that grew out of this counterculture movement was the most wholesome part of the Hippies' belief system. The 1969 Woodstock Concert (officially called "Woodstock Music & Art Fair") has been considered the "Counterculture National Convention." Museum at Bethel Woods 1960s museum is located at the historic site of the Woodstock festival and tells its story.

Many of the musicians who performed there played traditional folk music. Janis Joplin played a mix of blues done in her rock style, Country music had a spot where it mixed with psychedelic rock played by Country Joe McDonald who performed his "I-Feel-Like-I'm-Fixin'-To-Die Rag," a sarcastic Vietnam protest telling parents to send their sons off to war, so they could be the first on their block to get their boy back in a box.

Several others made it a place to have their protests heard. Joan Baez and Peter, Paul, and Mary were among the protesting musicians.

Creedence Clearwater Revival sang at Woodstock, but they didn't sing their protest song, "Fortunate Son." It's a punk rock sound and takes a stance against the war, stating how the rich wave the flag, but the poor go to war.

Jimi Hendrix, the most influential musician there, did a version of "The Star-Spangled Banner." His feedback, distortions seemed to imitate the sounds made by rockets and bombs. Analysts of the day claim his interpretation was a statement against the Vietnam War, however, in 2011 the editors of *Guitar World* named his performance of "The Star-Spangled Banner" the greatest performance of all time.

Bob Dylan began his career in high school under his birth name, Robert Allen Zimmerman, and played rock and roll. He listened to blues and country as well and was an avid fan of Woody Guthrie. He was also influenced by Pete Seeger. When Dylan moved to New York in 1961, he began visiting Guthrie at Creedmore State Hospital, where Guthrie died from Huntington's disease on October 3, 1967.

Dylan's second album, *The Freewheelin' Bob Dylan* with "Blowin' in the Wind" released in 1963, became the anthem for change in the '60s. He took the melody from the old spiritual "No More Auction Block" sung after England abolished slavery. When he sings about cannons needing to be silenced and men allowed to be free, the title implies that change is already beginning. The song is vague enough to be applied to any fight for freedom.

Another song in that album is pretty graphic. In "Masters of War," he wishes death upon those who build the weapons of war and profit from the death of innocent young men and destruction of the world.

Some words of "A Hard Rain's a-Gonna Fall" in the album referring to poison pellets falling in the water and scenes of death and despair throughout the song led people to believe it was written about the Cuban Missile Crisis from October 16 to October 28, 1962, when President Kennedy and Russian Premier Khrushchev were locked in a confrontation about US nuclear missiles in Italy and

Turkey and Russia countered by placing its nuclear missiles in Cuba. Since the song was written and released before the missile crisis, it clearly wasn't about that.

"Talkin' World War III Blues" takes a strangely humorous look at a dream of being one of the few people left alive after World War III.

"Oxford Town" deals with segregation. Specifically, James Meredith's enrollment at Mississippi State University in Oxford in 1961. Mississippi governor, Ross Barnett, refused to let a Black student be enrolled until President Kennedy issued a "cease and desist" order. Barnett was found to be in contempt and threatened with a $10,000 a day fine. Kennedy sent in the national guard, who finally enrolled Meredith, but not before two men were killed in the rioting. Dylan doesn't mention Meredith or the university by name, but it is pretty clear since there is only one university in Oxford. He does mention that the refusal to accept the student is because of the color of his skin. He suggests something be done about the deaths.

Dylan became involved both romantically and professionally with another singer prominent in the protest music era, Joan Baez. They sang together at the August 28, 1963 March on Washington demanding civil rights for all.

In Dylan's third album, *The Times They Are a-Changin'*, his songs took on civil rights very strongly. His title song told people, including politicians, if they would not help move thing forward to get out of the way. "Only a Pawn in Their Game" he refers specifically to the murder of civil rights worker Medgar Evers and lays the blame on the political hate speech that inspired the killing. Could we learn something from that song today?

He also deals with the double standard of one law for rich white people, and another for poor Black ones. In "The Lonesome Death of Hattie Carroll" he recounts the true story of the killing of black hotel barmaid Hattie Carroll, by young white socialite William Zantzinger. Zantzinger was duly tried and convicted by an all-white jury, then sentenced to six months in jail.

"Ballad of Hollis Brown" and "North Country Blues" dealt with the hardships faced by workers in farming and mining.

Moving into the late '60s, Dylan changed his style. He began performing more rock, and later did gospel. For most people old enough to remember his early work, he will always be remembered for his protest music.

In December 1997, US President Bill Clinton awarded Dylan a Kennedy Center Honor in the East Room of the White House. The president described Dylan thus: "Bob Dylan has never aimed to please. He's disturbed the peace and discomforted the powerful"

In 2016, The Nobel Prize committee awarded Dylan the Nobel Prize in Literature, the first musician to win the award, "for having created new poetic expressions within the great American song tradition."

Joan Baez began her career in 1959 with the opening track for the album *Folksingers 'Round Harvard Square*. She sang "Banks of the Ohio," a 19th-century murder ballad, similar to "Pretty Polly" or "Tom Dooley."

Baez met Bob Dylan at Gerde's Folk City in New York City's Greenwich Village in April 1961. They soon became romantically involved and worked together on many projects, especially protests. Baez would invite Dylan to sing on stage, either as a duet or on his own during her tours. They continued to collaborate professionally after their romantic relationship ended around 1965.

By 1963, Baez had released three albums, two of which had been certified gold. Her third album, *Joan Baez in Concert, Part 2*, was a second installment of live material, recorded during Joan Baez' concert tours of early 1963. It was the first of her albums to feature Bob Dylan cover songs, "Don't Think Twice It's Alright" and "With God on Our Side." It included the song fast becoming an anthem for the Civil Rights Movement, "We Shall Overcome." She recorded it for the album, at Miles College in Birmingham, Alabama, on the same day as the mass arrest of Civil Rights demonstrators in May 1963. The album hit at number 7 on the Billboard Pop Albums chart but, "With God on Our Side" got a lot of pushback from military proponents. The song is a sarcastic comment that since God is on our side, all of the atrocities like the Indian massacres by the army and the Civil War atrocities were right. It was quickly pulled from the album and replaced on the stereo version with more traditional folk songs, "Railroad Bill" and "Rambler Gambler."

Baez and Dylan performed the song live as a duet in July 1963 at the Newport Folk Festival. She again sang "We Shall Overcome" at the 1963 March on Washington for Jobs and Freedom and in Sproul Plaza during the mid-1960s Free Speech Movement demonstrations at the University of California, at Woodstock, and many other rallies and protests. Another song she sang that linked her to the Civil Rights Movement was "Birmingham Sunday," written by her brother-in-law, Richard Fariña, in 1964. The song tells of the four little girls killed in the Birmingham bombing and even mentions their names. It was used in the opening of Spike Lee's documentary film *4 Little Girls*. She also participated in the 1965 Selma to Montgomery marches for voting rights.

If you visit Birmingham today, there is a simple black stone monument on the side of the three-story, stone 16th Street Baptist Church telling more of the story. This was the site where four young girls lost their lives on Sunday, September 15, 1963. Addie Mae Collins, Cynthia Wesley, Carole Robertson, all 14 years old, and Carol Denise McNair, just 11 years old, were in the basement preparing for a choir performance that Sunday. A Klan bomb ended their young lives and injured twenty other parishioners.

Across the street in Kelly Ingram Park, there are sculptures depicting Birmingham's Civil Rights struggle. "Four Spirits," a life-sized sculpture on the corner directly across the street from 16th Street Baptist Church is of the four girls playing. I took Barry McNealy's Civil Rights Tour and recommend it highly when you visit Birmingham.

The Birmingham Civil Rights Institute is filled with the history of the struggle for equal rights from the 1950s through the '60s and into the present. So much of what the Civil Rights protest songs were about is displayed here.

Joan Baez was also an iconic figure in the anti-Vietnam-War movement. In 1964, she withheld sixty percent of her 1963 income taxes as a public resistance against the war. She met David Harris, founder of The Resistance, a protest group against the war, and a draft-resistance commune in the hills above Stanford, California. They married in March 1968. Just three months after their first meeting.

Harris had been drafted in January 1968 and refused. He was indicted almost immediately and charged with and tried in federal court in San Francisco in May 1968. He was convicted of felony "disobedience of a lawful order of induction" and sentenced to three years in prison. Harris was incarcerated in the Federal Prison System in July 1969 and where he spent twenty months before being paroled. After his release on March 15, 1971, Harris backed by Baez, continued protesting the Vietnam War until peace agreements were signed in March 1973. They became known as "Mr. and Mrs. Peace." However, after Harris' released Baez said, "things weren't the same between us." They divorced in 1973, but remained friendly and shared their son, Gabriel.

Joan Baez, her mother, and about 70 female protesters were arrested in October 1967, when they blocked doorways at the Oakland, California, Armed Forces Induction Center to prevent entrance by young inductees. They were incarcerated in the Santa Rita Jail.

Baez performed fourteen songs at the 1969 Woodstock Festival. She was the last act on the first day and closed with "We Shall Overcome."

On April 4, 2017, Baez released on her Facebook page her first new song in 27 years, "Nasty Man", a protest song against then President Trump, which became a viral hit. On April 7, 2017, she was inducted into the Rock and Roll Hall of Fame.

Buffy Sainte-Marie was one of the few full-blooded Native American to achieve success in music. She was born to Cree parents in 1941 on the Piapot 75 reserve in Saskatchewan, Canada. In a government attempt to destroy Indian culture, she was removed from her family and placed for adoption with a white family. She was adopted by an American couple from Wakefield, Massachusetts, Albert and Winifred Sainte-Marie. Her new family was sympathetic to Native culture and her adoptive mother privately claimed to be part Native American.

In 1963, when she saw wounded soldiers returning from Vietnam even though the US government claimed the US was not involved in the war, it inspired her protest song "Universal Soldier" on her debut album in 1964, *It's My Way,* on Vanguard Records. The song got her named Billboard magazine's Best New Artist. Much of her music dealt with the mistreatment of Native Americans, such as her 1964 songs, "Now That the Buffalo's Gone," and "My Country 'Tis of Thy People You're Dying."

Presidents Johnson and Nixon and FBI Director J. Edgar Hoover encouraged radio station to ban her after the release of these songs.

Peter, Paul and Mary formed in New York City in 1961. The trio consisted of Peter Yarrow, Paul Stookey, and Mary Travers. Like most folk singers of this era, they mixed popular folk ballads with their protest songs. The Weavers said Peter, Paul and Mary carried the torch of the social commentary of folk music in the 1960s. They covered many of the original Weavers songs written by Pete Seeger and Lee Hays.

Their first album, *Peter, Paul and Mary*, released in March 1962, did fantastic. It remained in Billboard Magazine's Top Ten for 10 months, with seven weeks at No. 1 position. Over time, it sold over two million copies and earned double platinum certification from the RIAA in the United States alone. Among the simple ballads, they included three songs protesting war and civil injustice. Member, Peter Yarrow co-wrote one of the war protests, "Cruel War," although the original version of the song dates back to the Civil war and possibly even to the Revolution. It tells of a woman who is so distraught when her lover is called to war that she wants to dress as a man and accompany him. "Where Have All the Flowers Gone?" was a cover of the Pete Seeger song. "If I Had a Hammer" was another Pete Seeger cover. It called for justice and love of our fellowman.

It was their second album, *Moving*, released in January 1963, that created quite an uproar. What the trio insist was a simple song about a young boy's coming of age triggered banning and controversy. "Puff, The Magic Dragon" talks about a dragon and a little boy's friendship until the boy grows up and forgets the dragon. The dragon cannot be happy without his friend and simply returns to his cave. The song was written by Peter Yarrow based on a poem his roommate at Cornell University in New York wrote in 1959 on Yarrow's typewriter. Yarrow shared writing credit with the roommate, Leonard Lipton, who also insists it is a poem about childhood innocence.

However, a 1964 Newsweek article claimed the song contained veiled references to smoking marijuana. They said "Puff" was a reference to taking a "puff" on a marijuana joint. The little boy's name, Jackie Paper, referred to rolling papers, "by the sea" where Puff Played in the song, supposedly stood for the C in cannabis, the "mist" stood for "smoke," and "dragon" was pronounced like "draggin'" (i.e., inhaling smoke). The land of "Honahlee" might have referred to the Hawaiian city of Hanalei, which is reputed to have some of the best marijuana in the world.

In 1970, vice-president Spiro Agnew wanted the song banned, along with pretty much all rock and roll music, as "blatant drug culture propaganda that threatened to sap our national strength unless we move hard and fast to bring it under control."

The song got attention and outrage in the media, and simultaneously achieving legendary status for getting on the radio at this time with such a clear reference to drugs. In spite of, or maybe because of, the massive mainline protest against it, "Puff The Magic Dragon" was a huge hit. The single reached number two on the Billboard Hot 100. The album charted at number two on Billboard's Pop Albums. Over the years, "Puff" has been covered by numerous other singers from Bing Crosby, The Andrews Sisters, Jackie De Shannon, The Irish Rovers, Connie Francis and others. In 1978, it was used in a movie about a little boy who couldn't speak until a magical dragon helped him find his voice. In 2007, Scholastic released an illustrated *Puff the Magic Dragon* children's book using the words of the song for the story.

Peter, Paul, and Mary broke up in 1970, to pursue solo careers but came together for a series of reunions and finally coming back together again. They played the Together for McGovern Concert at Madison Square Garden in support of George McGovern's presidential campaign, and again in 1978, for a concert protesting nuclear energy. In 1978 they held a summer reunion tour, after which they reunited until Mary's death in 2009.

Phil Ochs' "Talking Vietnam Blues" was "the first protest song to refer to Vietnam by name." His "What Are You Fighting For?" by talks about the many wrongs happening here in our own country and how we should right the wrongs at home before we take on other people's problems. In "I Ain't Marching Anymore" he talks about all the American wars the people the solder had killed and asks if is it worth it and that's why he's not marching anymore. When he sings "Too Many Martyrs" he mentions Medgar Evers and Emmett Till and that their only crime was their color. He comes on strong about fighting for freedom overseas while ignoring the racial murders here.

One of the most powerful protest songs was "Eve of Destruction" by **Barry McGuire** in 1965. It was his one and only hit but deserves mention. He asks how "Boy" cannot see that we are on the eve of destruction when you look at what is going on in the world with war, politicians, and the possibility of someone pushing the button to start a nuclear war. He tells listeners that if they think all the evil is in Red China, look at Selma, Alabama. Four people were killed and many more injured in the marches for civil right that year.

Of course many others we talked about in different genres also sang protest at injustice and war, like Nina Simone's "Ain't No Use," James Brown's "Say It loud—I'm Black and I'm Proud," Sam Cooke "A Change is Gonna Come," Marvin Gaye's "What's Going On," and others.

Exhibit about Woodstock at Musicians Hall of Fame in Nashville

Chapter 20 Muscle Shoals Sound

In the early '60s, in the northwest part of Alabama, a new genre emerged, The Muscle Shoals Sound. It's a sound that blends country, gospel and R & B, and is hard to define. Many of the artists who record here are famous in very different genres. Perhaps there is something in the water. The Native American who once lived there believed the Tennessee River sang to them. Maybe the best explanation is to paraphrase Waylon Jennings' statement in "Bob Wills is Still the King," You just can't play in Muscle Shoals if you don't have lots of soul.

The Muscle Shoals musical story began in 1959 when Rick Hall, Billy Sherrill and Tom Stafford founded Florence Alabama Music Enterprises in a small studio above City Drugstore in Florence, Alabama. Sherrill and Stafford dropped out of the business quickly.

Rick Hall moved to a former tobacco warehouse and then a building at 603 East Avalon in Muscle Shoals and renamed the business with the name's acronym, FAME Studio. Hall recorded all races there in spite of Jim Crow Laws. His white bands backed Black musicians. A big no-no then in the South.

Hall's first big hit in 1961 was Arthur Alexander's "You Better Move On." Hall continued to record musicians who later became stars like Wilson Pickett, Etta James, and Aretha Franklin. Franklin left the studio after one recording, "When a Woman Loves a Man," due to a fight between Hall and her husband, but she credits Hall for her becoming the "Queen of Soul." He recorded big name country singers like Shenandoah, Alabama, Pam Tillis, Tim McGraw, Billy Ray Cyrus, Reba McEntire, Bobby Gentry, Jerry Reed, and others.

Muscle Shoals Rhythm Section was FAME's basic backup band. They became known as "The Swampers" and are credited with creating a blend of R&B, soul and country music known as the "Muscle Shoals Sound."

One day, Hall invited a young homeless guitar player to play backup with the Swampers for Wilson Pickett. That was a starting point for the musician, Duane Allman, who went on to form The Allman Brother's

Band and create a new genre. Southern Rock was conceived at FAME. FAME Studio Is a working studio, but you can tour it.

In 1969, The Swampers split from FAME Studio over finances and founded a competing studio, **Muscle Shoals Sound Studio**. The backup band, Muscle Shoals Rhythm Section, opened their own studio called Muscle Shoals Sound Studio. "The Swampers" became the official name for the rhythm band when Lynyrd Skynyrd recorded there and used the name in the lyrics of "Sweet Home Alabama."

The four young men, Barry Beckett (keyboards), Jimmy Johnson (guitar), Roger Hawkins (drums), and David Hood (bass), rented an old building in Sheffield. It wasn't designed for a studio. It had a tin roof and whenever it rained, you can imagine what that did their sound effects. They ingeniously adapted it with makeshift sound proofing consisting of insulation and burlap. Cement block walls bounced sound around, but some Styrofoam from a friend helped add a layer of padding. It worked well enough that, in the nine years they used the building, they recorded 312 albums 75 that went gold, 14 platinum and over 100 top ten singles.

The studio was immortalized in 1969 on the cover of Cher's first solo album, "3614 Jackson Highway," also the first album cut at the studio.

They later moved to a newer building. They recorded the Rolling Stones, Willie Nelson, Paul Simon, Art Garfunkel, Bob Seegar, The Osmond Brothers, and many other big music names. Keith Richards called the area "rock-and-roll heaven" when the Rolling Stones recording at Muscle Shoals Sound Studios for three days. Muscle Shoals Sound Studio closed in 1979 and in 2013, the Muscle Shoals Music Foundation bought it and turned it into a touring opportunity and a working studio.

Alabama Music Hall of Fame showcases Alabama's most famous music icons. From Hank Williams to present day, it tells Alabama's music story. It's a fantastic museum. Some exhibits you might not connect with Alabama like Sun Studio in Memphis, Tennessee, but Sam Phillips, the studio owner who brought rock and roll to center stage, was from Florence.

Alabama's touring bus, The Solid Gold Country Music Car, is my favorite exhibit. This museum is a trip through Alabama's musical history.

The music history alone make Muscle Shoals area worth a trip but there is so much more to see here as well.

(Top) Fame Studio in Muscle Shoals, AL
(Bottom) Muscle Shoals Studio in Sheffield, AL

Chapter 21 Southern Rock

In 1969, The **Allman Brothers Band** you first met in Muscle Shoals combined the sounds of jazz, blues, and country music to create Southern Rock. In April 1969, the band's manager, Phil Walden, convinced the musicians to move to his home base in Macon, where he was trying to launch a new record label, Capricorn Records.

Today, Capricorn Studio was where so many other music legends, besides the Allman Brothers Band, recorded is reopened by Mercer University and combines a working studio with a museum. Its Studio A is where Southern Rock was born. Percy Sledge, Charlie Daniels, Wet Willie, and others recorded here as well.

Macon was already home to Otis Redding, Little Richard, and other music legends. Southern Rock made Macon the music hotbed of the country for a while. Duane Allman, who played slide guitar and lead guitar, brought in his brother, Gregg Allman, for vocals, keyboards, and songwriting. His other band members were Dickey Betts who played lead guitar, and did vocals and songwriting, Berry Oakley on bass, Butch Trucks on drums, and Jai Johanny "Jaimoe" Johanson, also on drums.

The Allman Brothers Band debuted in Jacksonville, Florida, on March 26, 1969, and released their first album, *The Allman Brothers Band*, in November 1969. They followed up with *Idlewild South* in 1970. Neither album was remarkable, with the most memorable songs being a cover of "Statesboro Blues" and "Midnight Rider" written by Gregg Allman and Robert Kim Payne and covered by many other singers, including Waylon Jennings. Their double album *At Fillmore East* was recorded live at the New York City music venue Fillmore East in 1971. It was well-received and pushed them to worldwide fame. The album, which had redos of songs on the first two albums, included several old blues numbers highly revved up, their "In Memory of Elizabeth Reed" and "Hot Lanta" were jamming instrumentals. Walden realized the Allman Brothers Band was at its best in concert, where they established contact with their followers rather than in a studio. Their music included blues, jazz, hard rock, and country music, and had bold ballads, heavy electric, and outlaw leanings.

On October 29, 1971,the band had begun recording their third studio album, *Eat a Peach*, when 24-year-old Duane Allman was killed in a motorcycle accident. At first, the band considered disbanding, but felt Duane would have wanted them to continue. Much of *Eat a Peach*'s songs revolve around Duane's death. The band played at his funeral and began touring again.

The band members had always been plagued by substance abuse, and after Duane's death, it grew worse. Oakely especially became more addicted. They released *Brothers and Sister* in 1973, and for many, the album still represents the pinnacle of Southern rock. During the recording of this album, Berry Oakley was killed in a motorcycle crash with a bus in Macon just blocks from where Duane died. You can visit both graves at Rose Hill Cemetery in Macon.

The band brought in Lamar Williams to replace Oakley, but the band began to disintegrate and eventually disbanded in 1976, shortly after a benefit for then presidential candidate Jimmy Carter. They reunited in 1979. It was never the same. Gregg was now involved with Cher, and the band permanently separated in 1982.

The Allman Brother's home in Macon, known as **The Big House**, is now open for tours. It's filled with instruments, clothing, memorabilia, and posters. The Big House was their home from 1970 to 1973 portions are furnished as it was when they lived there. The three-story twin-gabled house is one of Macon's newer museums. A painting of the band hangs next to their many gold records. The house is filled with the band's instruments and clothing. There are even notes where members composed many of their songs. Since The Allman Brothers Band campaigned for Jimmy Carter, one of their biggest fans, there are letters and information about him there.

Capricorn Studio, where Southern Rock was first recorded, sat deserted for many years. Finally, Mercer University brought about its rebirth. There is a small museum on the second floor. Downstairs, you can tour their working studio. Mercer Music at Capricorn director, Bob Konrad, showed us the new studio. He told us, "We built this studio in 2019. We're still a very active recording studio."

Then he led us across the lobby and showed us the original studio, a virtual shrine where so many famous musicians recorded in the 1970s. Besides the Allman Brothers Band, Lynyrd Skynyrd, Wet Willie, Charlie Daniels, and others recorded here. You can feel the old vibes there. Bob told us, "Everything here, except the instruments, is original."

For music lovers, the Rock Candy Tour in Macon is a must-do. Rock Candy Tours is co-owned by Jessica Walden, the daughter of Alan Walden and niece of Phil Walden, both inductees in the Georgia Music Hall of Fame and co-owners of the original Capricorn Records. She knows her music. The tour takes you to all the spots related to music around the city. My guide was Rex, who is so knowledgeable and seems to know lots of the local musicians as well as all his music facts.

While you are in Macon, stop and see the Douglass Theater and Grand Opera House where music of an earlier generation thrived.

Another group that led music into the Southern rock era was **Lynyrd Skynyrd** from Jacksonville and adjourning Clay County, Florida. Ronnie Van Zant, Allen Collins, Gary Rossington, Larry Junstrom, and Bob Burns formed Lynyrd Skynyrd in 1964. They first called themselves My Backyard, then Conquer the Worm for just a few days; they next tried The Noble Five, and finally The One Percent by 1968. In 1969, they became Lynyrd Skynyrd. They adopted the band's name from a former gym teacher at Westside Jacksonville's Robert E. Lee High School (now named Riverside High School). Leonard Skinner disliked boys having long hair and gave the members a hard time for that.

Lynyrd Skynyrd began as a part of the long-haired hippie counter culture. They were no friend to then President Nixon. Their use of the Confederate flag then was not a symbol of hate but a comment on their southern heritage. They are most known for hits like "Sweet Home Alabama" and "Free Bird." Band members Van Zant, Steve Gaines, and Cassie Gaines died in a plane crash in 1977. The band still plays with Ronnie's brother, Johnny, as lead singer, but there are no original members. The last surviving original band member guitarist Gary Rossington, died Sunday, March 5, 2023.

The band has moved from counter culture to conservative in later years. They practiced in Clay County since they couldn't rehearse in Jacksonville because the police would get called about them disturbing the peace with the loud noises. Their rehearsal studio was a tiny wooden cabin out in the woods by a creek. The cabin had electricity and running water, but no air conditioning, so they nicknamed it "Hell House." The cabin is long gone. Today, the gated community of Edgewater Landing stands there.

Ronnie Van Zant Memorial Park is dedicated to his memory and is a great place to hike or let kids play. If you get hungry for some seafood, Whitey's Fish Camp on Fleming Island, Ronnie's favorite dining spot, is not far away on Doctor's Lake. Ronnie and Gary fished here during the 1970s Pepsi Cola *Tribute to Lynyrd Skynyrd* video's opening shots. Whiteys' dock is also featured in *Freebird: The Movie*. Whiteys is just a short distance from Ronnie's former home on Brickyard Road, where he was living at the time of the plane crash.

In Jacksonville there are markers by their childhood home of the Van Zant family, and two residences, The Gray House and The Green House, once occupied by members of the Allman Brothers Band. The Van Zant Home is now an Airbnb.

Allman Brothers Band Exhibit at The Big House in Macon, GA

Lynyrd Skynyrd exhibit at Alabama Music Hall of Fame in Muscle Shoals, AL

(Top) Studio at Capricorn Studio (Bottom) Dock at Whitey's Fish Camp, Ronnie Van Zant's favorite hangout and fishing spot in Fleming Island, FL

Chapter 22 Pop

What was the first pop song ever made? Definitions all over the board. American folk singer Pete Seeger defined pop music as "professional music which draws upon both folk music and fine arts music."

Some say the first major pop song was "After the Ball" because it was the first song to sell millions of copies of sheet music. It was written in 1891 and debuted in 1892 by Charles Harris. It's a classic waltz in 3/4 time originally written for a Milwaukee, Wisconsin amateur minstrel show. Its popularity boomed when John Philip Sousa and his band performed it at the 1893 World's Fair in Chicago.

The term pop music originated in the late 1940s and early 1950s to describe music from a blend of jazz, swing, blues, and country. It describes songs that gained popularity due to its catchy melodies, lyrics that resounded with listeners, and simple musical arrangements.

The term "pop" is short for popular, or the music favored by the public. It became common usage in the middle of the 20th century. It's hard to fit a song or musician into this as a lot of music in all genres is popular. So I'm including here those that didn't fit distinctly into one other genre.

Another classic America song was only half American. John Howard Payne and English composer Sir Henry Bishop wrote "Home, Sweet Home" in 1823 for an opera that was first produced in London. The song became hugely popular throughout the United States. During the Civil War, it was a favorite of both sides. With lyrics including "Be it ever so humble, there's no place like home," it's easy to see why.

The first major American popular songwriter, **Stephen Foster,** wrote sentimental songs for the minstrel era. Although most minstrel songs dehumanized African Americans, Foster wrote more compassionately than most songwriters of the period, such as in "Nelly Was a Lady," he sings about a black man mourning the loss of his wife. Foster's 1851 "Old Folks at Home" also known as "Way Down Upon the

Swanee River," became a huge national hit. It's still the Florida State Song, but in 2008, the lyrics were revised to change "plantation" to "station," and the Black dialect has been changed to standard English.

Things changed when recording became possible, early in the 20th century. Music could be much more widely disseminated. Records were relatively cheap. Just as happened in The Bristol Sessions, music of all genres became universally played on records. That opened a market for professional songwriters in New York who turned out fast pieces intended to be recorded by others. It was called Tin Pan Alley. Most of what they wrote was just gimmicky trash, but they occasionally produced some beautiful material. Jack Norworth and Albert von Tilzer wrote "Take Me Out to the Ball Game," one of my dad's all-time favorites. Irving Berlin wrote "God Bless America" and "White Christmas." Hughie Cannon and Johnnie Queen created "Bill Bailey, Won't You Please Come Home." Some of the other memorable names who wrote Tin Pan Alley songs included George M. Cohan, George Gershwin, Ira Gershwin, Oscar Hammerstein II, Jerome Kern, Frank Loesser, and Cole Porter.

The early 1900s were a time of vaudeville, barbershop quartets and crooners. One of the most successful crooners was **Bing Crosby**. Crosby was influenced by Al Jolson, who performed vaudeville and minstrel. Jolson was one of the highest-paid stars of the 1920s.

Crosby's biggest hit was his version of **Irving Berlin**'s "White Christmas." He was also the singer of another of my dad's favorites, "I Found a Million Dollar Baby (in a Five and Ten Cent Store)."

Pop music exploded during this period, since the low price of records created greater demand and more profits for the record industry. Music marketing became common, creating a number of mainstream pop stars. Many Italian-American crooners like **Dean Martin**, **Rudy Vallee**, **Tony Bennett**, **Perry Como**, **Frankie Laine**, and **Frank Sinatra** were at the forefront.

Frank Sinatra was the first to create havoc, much as Elvis would a generation later, with millions of screaming teenaged girls wherever he went. He was called "Chairman of the Board" and "Ol' Blue Eyes." The fact that he was reputed to have Mafia connections only added to his legend. Sinatra was one of the most popular entertainers throughout the 1940s, 1950s, and into the 1960s. He has sold an estimated 150 million records.

Sonny & Cher hit their stride in the 1960s and 1970s, made up of spouses, Cher and Sonny Bono. The couple started their career in the mid-1960s as R&B backing singers for record producer Phil Spector.

Their biggest claim to fame were two hit songs in 1965, "Baby Don't Go" and "I Got You Babe". The couple's career as a duo ended in 1975 following their divorce. She later married Greg Allman.

Cher went on to an ongoing successful career as a solo artist. "If I Could Turn Back Time" and "Believe" are her biggest hit.

Bruce Springsteen, known as "The Boss" recorded his first album *Greetings from Asbury Park, N.J.*, in January 1973, Right on the cusp of what I am considering the modern age. Neither that nor his second, *The Wild, the Innocent & the E Street Shuffle*, got much of a following.

It was with his third album, *Born to Run,* in 1975 that he hit his stride. When he released *Born in the USA* in 1984, it became one of the best-selling albums of all time. His title song might have fit in the protest era as it was protesting the poor treatment of Vietnam Veterans in their search for jobs. Ironically, President Ronald Reagan must have only heard the title and not the words as he seemed to embrace the song and referred to it as a "message of hope." Springsteen commented at a concert a few days later that he didn't know what album the president could be listening to. He then began to play "Johnny 99," a song about a factory worker being laid off when an auto factory shut down and was arrested and sentenced to prison for 99 years for waving a gun around because he was desperate about losing his home, since he couldn't pay the mortgage.

In modern times, Madonna, Prince, and Michael Jackson, were cultural icons. Michael Jackson was known as the "King of Pop," he is regarded as one of the most significant cultural figures of the 20th century. His dance, the Moonwalk, remains an American Classic. You already met him in Motown where he began his career as part of The Jackson Five. This is the history of American music. Modern music is more global and would take an entire new book.

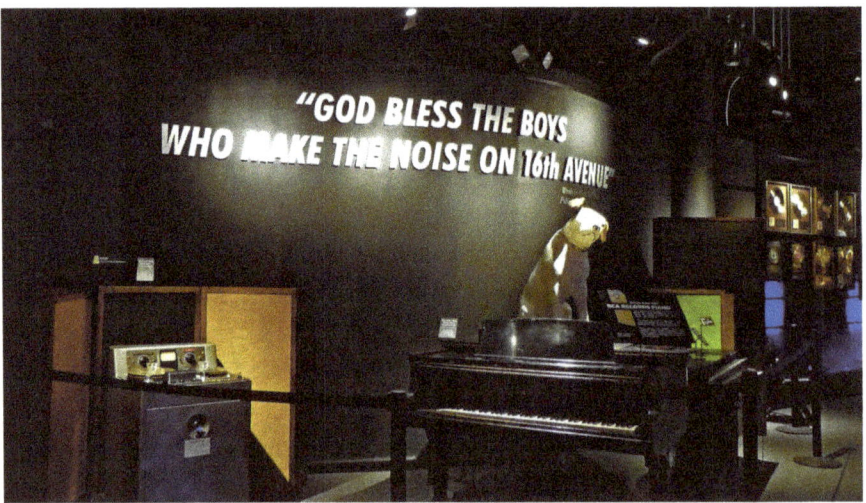

(Top) My Rock Candy Tour guide points out what was Le Bistro where Greg Allman proposed to Cher in Macon, GA (Bottom) The Musicians Hall of Fame in Nashville recognizes all genres of musicians

Photo of Cher and Muscle Shoals crew after she recorded her first solo album

Index

100 Man Hall	32	Carl and Pearl Butler	75
Aaron Neville	151	Carter Family Fold	73
Alabama Music Hall of Fame	205	Charley Pride	87
Allen Toussaint	148, 150	Charlie Parker	64
Allman Brothers Band	28, 207	Cher	205, 208, 215
American Banjo Museum	11	Cheraw	56
Amédé Ardoin	17	Chubby Checker	86, 144, 167
Anderson Music Hall	108	Clarksdale	24, 26, 36, 144
Andrew Johnson Hotel	75	Cleveland	17, 77, 164, 166, 174
Aretha Franklin	22, 141p1, 145, 179, 204	Cléoma Breaux	14
		Clifton Chenier	17
Augusta Museum of History	145	Clintwood	118, 121
Axe Handle Distillery	119	Clyde McPhatter	144
B. B. King	30pp163, 37, 126	Columbus	27p1, 34
B. B. King Museum	30	Congo Square	11p1, 48
Baker's Keyboard Lounge	49	Country Music Hall of Fame	86p1, 100p1, 110, 113, 175
ballads	3	countrypolitan	113
Bay St. Louis	32	Cradle of Country Music	76
Bayou Delight	16	Creedence Clearwater Revival	196
Bayou Teche Brewing	18	Creole Nature Trail Adventure Point	18
Beale Street	27, 171	Crooked Road	9, 72p1
Benny Goodman	4	Dahlonega	9p1
Berry Gordy, Jr.	157	Dean Martin	214
Bessie Smith	22, 26p1	DeFord Bailey	77
Billie Holiday	60, 190	Delta Blues Museum	26
Bing Crosby	4, 47, 77, 214	DeSoto County Museum.	32
Birmingham	61, 67, 198p1	DeSoto Museum	38
Blairsville	5p1, 8p1, 125p1	Detroit	29, 145, 157, 174
Blind Willie McTell	28, 77	Dick Clark	167
Blue Moon	16, 119, 171	Dizzy Gillespie	4, 63pp163
Blue Ridge Institute & Museum	9	Dockery Farm	24
Bo Diddley	178p1	Dolly Parton	7, 28, 105, 110pp163
Bob Dylan	139, 196, 198	Dollywood	112
Bob Wills	100p1, 171	Don Gibson	86
Bobby Gentry	115	Don Gibson Theater	86
Booker T. & the M.G.'s	142	Douglas Theater	209
Boswell Sisters	4, 61p1	Dr. John	148pp163
Bristol Sessions	68p1, 128	Earl Scruggs	119
Brownsville	180	Earl Scruggs Center	120
Bruce Springsteen	215	Edith Dickens	120
Buck and Johnny's	18	Emmylou Harris	111
Buddy Holly	181	Ernest Hogan	41
Buffy Sainte-Marie	200	Ernest Tubb	74, 78p1, 100
Burger Bar	80	Etta James	147
Butcher Holler	110	Eva Davis	9
Cab Callaway	143	Everly Brothers	87pp163, 165
Cajun music	14pp163	FAME Studio	205
Call and Response	12, 21p1	Faron Young	85
Capricorn Studio	177, 207	Ferriday	174
		Festivals Acadiens et Créoles	18

Fisk Jubilee Singers	136	Kenny Rogers	102
Florida Theater	172	Kentucky	41, 108, 110, 119, 171
Floyd, Virginia	9	Kitty Wells	83, 86, 104p1
Floyd's General Store	9	Kris Kristofferson	122, 125
Four Tops	158p1	Lafayette	14, 16, 131
Frank Sinatra	214	Lake View Cemetery	167
Frankie Laine	214	Lester Flatt	119
Gainesville	179	Little Richard	141p1, 176p1, 207
Gateway to the Blues	24	Loretta Lynn	4, 79, 105, 107pp163, 115, 118
Gatorland	113		
Geechee	13	Louis Armstrong	45pp163, 60, 63, 69p1, 176
Gene Autry	85, 98pp163		
George Jones	68, 74, 114, 182	Louis Jordan	142
Georgetown	13	Louisiana	11, 14pp163, 83pp163, 101, 171, 174p1, 178
Grand Ole Opry	72, 74p1, 77pp163, 83, 100p1, 119, 130, 138, 169pp163		
		Lum York	80
Grandaddy Mimms Distilling Company	125p1	Lynyrd Skynyrd	4, 209
		Ma Rainey	22, 27p1
Grapelle Butt Mock House	8	Macon	75, 176p1, 207p1
Gray House	210	Macon, Georgia	176
Ground Zero Blues Club	26, 36	Mahalia Jackson	137
Gullah	13	Mamie Smith	25
Hank Ballard	144	Martha and the Vandellas	159
Hank Williams Museum	80	Marty Robbins	83, 102
Harry Choates	16	Marvin Gaye	145
Hiawassee	108	Mary Wells	159
Howlin' Wolf	24, 28p1	Mavis Staples	139
Icky's	110	Memphis	25, 27, 29pp163, 142, 164, 169pp163, 183
Ike Turner	26, 29, 167p1, 179p1, 183		
Indianola	24, 30, 32, 36	Michael Jackson	159, 162, 215
International Sweethearts of Rhythm	59	Minnie Pearl	74, 77, 107
Irving Berlin	214	Mississippi	17, 21, 23p1, 26, 29pp163, 39, 59, 67, 69p1, 113, 144, 164, 170, 174p1
Isaac Hayes	142, 153		
Jack Scott	167		
Jacksonville	172, 207, 209	Montgomery	79p1, 82p1
James Brown	144	Motown	145, 157, 160p1
Janis Joplin	181p1	Muddy Waters	24, 26, 29, 164, 179
jazz	4, 11, 42, 59pp163, 68p1, 78, 100, 136, 142p1, 166p1, 177, 207	Muscle Shoals	204p1, 207
		Muscle Shoals Sound Studio	205
Jelly Roll Morton	42, 44, 46, 78	Museum of East Tennessee History	75
Jerry Lee Lewis	32, 169, 174, 176	Museum of the Gulf Coast	181
Jimi Hendrix	4, 183	Musicians Hall of Fame	88
Jimmie Buffett	88	Nashville	74, 77, 83, 85, 87, 100, 104p1, 107, 110pp163, 122
Jimmy Dickens	77		
Jimmy Rodgers	69, 85	Nashville Songwriters Hall of Fame	102
Joe Falcon	14		
John Lee Hooker	32	Neville Brothers	151
Johnny Cash	69, 79, 107, 122, 128pp163, 169pp163	New Orleans	4, 11, 14, 24p1, 32, 39, 42, 61, 101, 136, 148, 177p1
Katy Depot Museum	40	New Orleans Jazz Museum	48
Kelly Ingram Park	199	North Carolina	13, 70, 120

Oakwood Cemetery Annex	80
Oklahoma City	11, 101
Old Mint	48, 178
Olivia Newton-John	111
Otis Redding	141p1, 176, 207
Patsy Cline Museum	105, 107
Penn Center	13
Perry Como	214
Peter Seeger	191, 194
Peter, Paul and Mary	201
Phil Ochs	202
Pigeon Forge	112
Port Arthur	17, 181
Preservation Hall	48
Professor Longhair	148p1
R&B	66, 136, 141pp163, 166pp163, 178
race music	136
ragtime	25, 39pp163, 61, 166
Ralph Peer	68, 128
Ralph Stanley	119
Ralph Stanley Museum	118, 121
Ray Charles	143
RCA Studio B	87
Reba McEntire	204
Rhythm and Blues	17, 66, 136, 141, 145, 166, 168, 174, 176, 178p1
Ritchie Valens	181
Robert Johnson	22pp163, 35
Rock and Roll Hall of Fame	63, 139, 146, 164, 175, 178, 182
Roy Rogers	99p1
Rudy Vallee	214
Ryman Auditorium	74, 77
Sam Cooke	144
Scott Joplin	39p1
Scott Joplin House	43
Shelby	120
Shenandoah Memorial Park	107
Shreveport	85, 101, 171
Sister Rosetta Tharpe	136, 166
Smokey Robinson	157p1
Sonny & Cher	215
Soul music	141pp163
South Carolina	13
Southern Rock	105, 207
St. Augustine	11
St. Augustine Amphitheater	134
St. Helena	13
Statesboro	28
Stax	142, 145, 88, 139
Stephen Foster	213
Sulfur	18
Sun Studio	29, 169p1, 183
Tammy Wynette	4, 113
Tennessee	31, 68, 70, 75, 83, 100, 107, 109p1, 112, 114, 130, 180
Tex Ritter	99p1
Tex Ritter Park	182
Texas	17, 39, 70, 78, 83p1, 99pp163, 174, 181p1
The Big Bopper	69, 181
The Big House	208
The Birmingham Civil Rights Institute	199
The Crossroads	23
The Marvelettes	158
The Miracles	158
The Musicians Hall of Fame	88
The Supremes	158
The Temptations	161
The Texas Country Music Hall of Fame	182
Thomas A. Dorsey	136
Thomas M. Turpin	40
Tina Turner	179pp163
Tipitina's	149
Tony Bennett	214
Tony Jackson	42
Tupelo	164, 170p1
Vermillionville	16
Victor Young	4
Virginia	9, 11, 61p1, 72, 77, 105p1, 113, 118pp163
Vogel State Park	9
W. C. Handy	22, 25, 27
Waylon Jennings	87, 122p1, 125
Webb Pierce	83, 85, 104
West Tennessee Delta Heritage Center	180
West Virginia	61, 77, 120
Whitney Houston	111
Willie Nelson	105, 122p1, 125pp163, 143
Willie Nelson and Friends Museum	128
Winchester	105p1
WNOX	75
Woody Guthrie	194
zydeco	14, 16pp163
"Aunt" Samantha Bumgarner	9
"Buddy" Bolden	44
"Sleepy John" Estes	180